Printed in the United States of America

ISBN: 1519675976

ISBN-13: 978-1519675972

CREDITS

Proofreader	Erin Hemme Froslie
Cover & Interior Design	Cassia Ward *Graphic Designer*
Author Photographer	John Borge *John Borge Studios*

PRAISE FOR
"LIFE BY DESIGN"

"Teresa Lewis has written a remarkable book that answers the questions we all have about how to live our best life. Millions of people are drifting through life wondering if this is as good as it gets. Well, life is too short to live someone else's dreams. Teresa masterfully shares how to live your own life - one filled with passion, purpose and intention. Life by Design is an inspirational and empowering book that captures your heart, stimulates your mind, and brings joy to your soul. The only thing better than reading Teresa's new book is listening to her speak about it."

Scott Shickler
Bestselling Author & Cofounder
The 7 Mindsets

"Teresa Lewis is well known on the speaking platform encouraging her audiences to make changes and adjustments to their busy and chaotic lives, slowing the pace to live more intentionally and on purpose. As the reader turns the pages, there is a stirring and an urgency to examine one's own life and make changes and shifts where necessary to live life by design instead of by default. Her words evoke a sense of vulnerability in an imperfect life as she mindfully shares stories of impact on her life's journey. Sprinkled with the perfect amount of humor, it is a wonderful read for those who wish to live life at a deeper level. Teresa's writings deliver a powerful punch of takeaways to implement immediately. This book is a fabulous companion piece for those who hear her on stage and a perfect introduction for others who have not yet had the chance to hear her live."

Reneé Rongen
International Inspirational Speaker,
Award-Winning Author and Life Strategist

"Simply brilliant. With this book, Teresa Lewis has done what very few can. She succinctly communicates the opportunities we all have to improve the design of our lives, make the most of our circumstances, and move forward toward our goals, dreams and aspirations. If your desire is to take your

life to the next level, the stories, humor and wisdom printed on these pages are all you'll need. Read this book, share it with your friends ... in doing so, you'll change the world."

Mark J. Lindquist
Motivational Speaker

"Teresa Lewis has shared her journey, along with the lessons she has learned that are both real and relatable. This book will inspire you to live life more intentionally and find more peace along the journey. Whether you're dreaming big dreams or you are looking for a resource to help you get to a better place, this book is for you!"

Missy Ohe
The Ohepen Mind
Certified John Maxwell Speaker

CONTENTS

LESSONS I'VE LEARNED ON MY JOURNEY THAT CAN HELP YOU WITH YOURS

DEDICATION

This book is dedicated to my family, whose love, laughter and support is essential every day.

My husband, Steve, has always supported me. He's had more confidence in me than I have, and it was his urging that helped me launch my business. He dreams big, takes risks and has helped me keep moving forward.

Our firstborn, Alyssa, has grown up to become an independent and smart young lady, in spite of our parenting fails as we raised her. Her book smarts and street smarts will take her far ... just hopefully not too far away. We love having family close.

Our youngest, Tara, provides lots of humor. A few years ago, Tara mentioned she wanted a book dedicated to her. When I told her I was writing a book, she assured me she didn't want *my book* dedicated to her, she wanted a dedication by someone *famous*. (This will have to do for now, Tara!)

I'm grateful to my parents, Tom and Bonnie Fosse, for always supporting me. When I told my mom I was quitting my job to become self-employed, she said, "Your dad would have been proud of you." My dad passed away in 2005 and, as you'll see, his life played a big role in me pursuing my passions.

My in-laws, George and Edna Mae Lewis, give in-laws a good name. They're always willing to drop everything and help, which we've really appreciated throughout the years.

I give my greatest thanks to God, from whom all blessings flow.

SETTING THE STAGE

PRIMER

This book was created to help you get more intentional with your life. It's not a step-by-step guide, it's not a checklist. It contains a bit of my story (first section) and lessons learned on my journey (second section) to help you with yours. I really didn't plan to include "my story," but it's very common to have audience members talk to me after a keynote and ask how I became a speaker. The answer to that question isn't necessarily simple and it's been a journey, so I decided to share some of it here.

I'd like to challenge you to *give yourself time to think* as you read this. Yes, time to think! What a concept! One of Google's chief executives, Eric Schmidt, has stated that our instantaneous devices are having a negative impact on our thought process – obstructing deep thinking and making learning more difficult. That's a bit ironic coming from a Google executive, isn't it?

It is true. We have so many gadgets, distractions, and interruptions that deep thinking can be a challenge for many of us. So, I challenge you … take time to think and reflect. You'll be glad you did.

"Thinking is the hardest work there is. That's why so few people engage in it."
- Henry Ford

INSTANT GRATIFICATION

Let's face it; we live in an age of instant gratification. Pressing a button on our phone enables us to be face-to-face with someone on the other side of the planet; we can Google any question for an immediate (and sometimes accurate) answer; and we can order virtually anything online and have it on our doorstep the following day.

We have that mentality, yet we know that most worthwhile pursuits in life take time. Exercise pays off, just not immediately. Eating well pays off, just not immediately. Persistent effort toward a worthy goal pays off, just not immediately. We know this; we just don't always appreciate this.

Here is something that can appease our desire for instant gratification; *shifting your mindset yields immediate results*. As you dig into this book, you'll see that much of it relates to mindset.

Shifting your mindset can change your life and impact the lives of those around you.

SELF-HELP GETS A BAD RAP

You might label this book as a self-help book, and, of course, a lot of people make fun of self-help. In my view, the opposite of self-help is self-sabotage. If you aren't on board with self-help, are you a fan of self-sabotage? As someone with strong faith, I know it is not only up to me; God is ultimately in control. Nonetheless, I still have to do my part, so God can do His. I know I need a lot of help, so if I can help myself along the journey, then I most certainly will. I've learned that if I am not striving to be the best person I can be, I am probably sabotaging my efforts. My purpose on earth is to make a positive and profound impact, so shouldn't I do everything within my control to make that happen?

WHY THE WORLD NEEDS THIS BOOK

Life is not all gumdrops and lollipops, not by a long shot. It never will be, and, generally speaking, we aren't handling that fact well. Let's look at a few statistics that indicate how well we are living life, just to state the case that most of us could benefit from living intentionally.

Disengaged at Work

Approximately 100 million people in the U.S. hold full-time jobs. Of those, according to Gallup.com, about 30 million (30%) are *engaged* and inspired at work. The rest are either *disengaged* (50%) or, worse, *actively disengaged* (20%).

The Gallup research also indicates that having too few engaged employees results in workplaces that are less safe, have more quality defects, and have higher healthcare costs.*

Not Very Happy

In the U.S. we are blessed with opportunity, knowledge, and freedom. Yet, only one in three Americans said they are "very happy," according to a 2013 Harris Poll. Just look around at the grocery store and you'll see evidence of this – so many scowls, so much rushing, so much frustration.**

Worried. Anxious.

We are worriers. Too much worry can result in an array of anxiety disorders. Anxiety disorders are the most common mental illness in the U.S.,

*Source: Gallup www.gallup.com
**Source: Harris Interactive www.harrisinteractive.com

affecting 18% of adults. And, the majority of anxiety sufferers are women.*

This was hugely evident at an event I attended along with about 4,500 others in August 2015. It was a Beth Moore Living Proof Live event and the focus was anxiety. Beth asked us to rate our experience with anxiety on a scale of 1-4, with 1 being "I'm rarely impacted by anxiety" and 4 being "Anxiety is one of the biggest problems in my life." The overwhelming majority of the audience voted on the high end - anxiety was either a 3 or 4 in their life and it greatly impacted them on a regular basis.

Less Optimistic

We've become less optimistic. According to a Gallup poll, there has been a general decline in optimism levels in the U.S.; in 2013 only 67% of respondents said that they were optimistic about the future, as compared to 75% in 2011. And, optimism levels in the U.S. are significantly below the global average; internationally 89% of citizens feel optimistic about the future.**

---

*Source: National Institute of Mental Health www.nimh.nih.gov

**Source: Gallagher, M. W., Lopez, S. J. and Pressman, S. D. (2013), Optimism Is Universal: Exploring the Presence and Benefits of Optimism in a Representative Sample of the World. Journal of Personality, 81: 429–440. doi: 10.1111/jopy.12026

Addictions

Substance abuse continues to be a problem in the U.S. and illicit drug use continues to climb. Drug overdose death rates have increased in many states in recent years. It's estimated that over 23 million Americans struggle with addiction, yet only 1% of those individuals receive treatment.*

Suicide

Every day, approximately 105 people in the U.S. die from suicide. Lives lost to suicide are more than double lives lost to homicide.**

First World Problems

We have more choices than we've ever had. We have so many choices that we get overwhelmed and find it difficult to actually make a decision.

We try to control that which we can't; we don't take control of that which we can.

We have more possessions, but fewer values.

We have more access to more information, but fewer reflective thoughts.

---

*Source: National Institute on Drug Abuse www.drugabuse.gov
**Source: Suicide Awareness Voices of Education www.save.org

Happiness is Elusive

For the most part, we're educated, we're talented, we strive for happiness, but why is it so elusive? Here are my thoughts:

We rely on others for our happiness. Of course, others can bring us happiness and joy, but once we start relying on other people for our happiness, we are setting ourselves up for disappointment.

We don't allow ourselves to be happy now; we think we can only be happy at some future point after everything falls into place.

We compare ourselves to others and always fall short. We don't see the entirety of their lives, just as they don't see the whole picture of ours. The irony is that THEY probably think WE have it all together, too!

We don't appreciate the little blessings in life. Instead, we take too much for granted.

We'd rather be right than be happy. We want so badly to prove we are right that we alienate those around us. We justify our behavior to prove our point and satisfy our ego instead of sharing a simple apology when one is due.

We are spending money we don't have on things we don't need to impress people we don't know. It's exhausting.

That's why this book is necessary.

The reality behind those facts and statistics can be hard to digest. In addition to these disturbing stats, it's apparent that too many people are simply going through the motions and not living (or even seeking) their best life.

The great news is that each of us individually can do our part in living life intentionally so we can make a positive impact on others.

WHERE ARE YOU?

Waiting for Your Ship to Come In?

"It's so great that your ship came in!" This is what a co-worker told me when I shared the news that I was quitting my job to launch my own business. Your ship has come in. Picture that in your mind: A beautiful yacht ready to sail you to tropical and exotic destinations.

If only that were the case.

In reality, quitting my corporate job (you know the type with the nice, steady paycheck and great benefits) to venture out on my own was

"You can never cross the ocean unless you have courage to lose sight of the shore."

- Christopher Columbus

more about me swimming out to find my ship. And, swimming out to find my ship involved jumping off a really high cliff into some very turbulent waters.

There have been times that I've needed the life preservers thrown to me. There have been times I've felt like the waves would overtake me. Those are the times that it is critical to keep going.

Are you going through the motions while you're waiting for your ship to come in? Are you waiting for the perfect opportunity and the perfect timing before you take the next step? If you wait for the conditions to be perfect, you might be waiting a long time; in fact, you might be waiting your whole life.

What does your ship look like? Is it taking on more responsibility at work? Is it getting that degree? Acquiring new skills to qualify for that promotion? Taking a leap and starting a business? Signing up for that class that you've always wanted to take? Giving back in a bigger way?

May this book give you the courage to take a step in that direction.

Is Everything "Fine"?

Maybe you don't have an addiction, maybe you don't abuse substances, maybe your life is "fine" ... but what if "fine" isn't the goal? When life is "fine," you can stay there for a long time. Life there is not necessarily painful. When life gets painful, then it's pretty easy to realize you want change, need change and are ready to take steps to change. When life is "fine," it's easy to coast.

Don't wait for your ship to come in. Swim out to get it.

I believe being on a path of "fine" will take you to a well-known place called "complacency." Complacency is a place I've visited but have no desire to return to. Remember those Gallup polls? Complacency is where the majority of the American workforce is.

A little spark of fire, a spark of inspiration ... that can be enough to ignite one soul, then another, then another. The spark you ignite within yourself could be contagious.

"The only time you coast is when you are going downhill."

- Dennis Seeb

On the Verge?

Have you ever had the feeling that you were on the verge of something, but you didn't know what? When I experienced that feeling, I didn't know what it meant or what to do about it. I didn't know *what* I was on the verge of or how I could even identify that feeling, but I felt it. I started taking steps,

"You only need a spark to start a whole blaze. It only takes a little faith."

- Lyrics from "Start a Fire" by Unspoken

reading personal development books, writing, reflecting, attending retreats. I gave myself time and space to evaluate what was working, what wasn't, and what was missing. Those steps created momentum in my life. And, eventually, I discovered what I was on the verge of. It didn't happen overnight, but every step I've taken has acted like a flashlight illuminating my path.

Just Getting Through It?

A friend told me she had so much to do before her daughter's wedding that she couldn't wait for it to be over. "If only I could just get through the next few months." How often have you said that, "I just want to get through x, y, or z (the holidays, that exam, that project, this stage)"? Guess what? Your life is made up of the stages, the holidays, the exams, and the projects. Do you really want to *just get through it*? Think about those battling a terminal illness; they want to savor each day and not miss a moment. Meanwhile, your "busy-ness" is ruling your life, and you just want to skip over these days and fast forward a week or a month. That phrase is like an early warning alarm that it's time to slow down, take a breath, and evaluate *why* you are doing what you are doing.

"People say motivation doesn't last. Neither does bathing, that's why we recommend it daily."

- Zig Ziglar

Let's be real - sometimes life throws you a curveball and it IS about getting through it. Believe me, I get it. As I was nearing the end of writing this book, I went through a cycle of cluster headaches. In times of excruciating pain, yes, maybe it is about getting through it. When you're going through the grieving process after the loss of a loved one, maybe it is about getting through it.

Feel Like You're the Only One?

In the Midwest over the winter months, it's common to hear people talk about the "wind chill factor" (how chilly it really feels once you add the wind to the already cold temps). Well, in a humble state, I'll admit that for years I lived under the notion that this was the "windshield factor." Once I learned the correct terminology, you can bet I kept this newfound revelation to myself; I was certain no one on the face of the earth had ever been that ignorant! Imagine my delight as I overheard a conversation on a particularly cold day in the Rockies as I was writing this book. The server was telling a restaurant patron that she used to think "wind chill factor" was called "windshield factor." Yes, I can relate to that; I can relate to her; I suddenly don't feel alone.

Wherever you are now, my wish is that this book inspires and encourages you to take steps toward your best life, a life by design.

Have you ever felt like that? Like you're the only one who doesn't have it all together? Like you're the only one who has ever had such an internal battle? Like you're the only one who has ever felt like *this*?

You are never alone. It may feel like it, but you are never alone. Others are there; others have been there; and others will be there. Those who have made it through become trailblazers for those who are going through it.

Want to Be Better Tomorrow Than Today?

Maybe you're on a path of continual improvement, because you know that once you stop improving yourself, you can go downhill quickly. Congratulations for keeping on. It takes perseverance and discipline, and that's not always easy.

MY LIFE

Many people have pretty incredible stories. They have overcome poverty, homelessness, abuse and other tough situations and eventually written books, shared their message with thousands and given others hope. I've never experienced difficulties or tragedies in those forms, thank God. At one point, I even thought my future would be limited because I hadn't experienced trials of that magnitude. I'm over that now (trust me, I don't feel any need to be homeless or to develop an addiction). I've come to realize that the lessons I've learned and the obstacles I've overcome may resonate with you. Whether the obstacles in front of you seem like road bumps or insurmountable mountains, I hope this book helps. My wish is that the lessons I've learned along my journey will help you with your journey.

This is about getting intentional with your life, so you can live a life by design, not default. I lived by default for years, especially in my professional life. Let's not label that as bad; I've had a ton of fun, great experiences and wonderful memories. Everything that I've experienced until now has created who I am today. I just wasn't intentional about my life.

I was letting life happen to me.

Everything you've experienced so far has created who you are today.

I unwittingly lived life by default for years. It's no one's fault, I just didn't know any better. All my life experiences have made me the person I am today, so it's not about commiserating what could have been. It's more about knowing I could have impacted more people earlier in life if I had figured this out earlier. And, please understand, I don't have it all figured out yet, this is just where I am on my journey. No matter what stage you are at, I truly hope this book helps you *now*.

IN THE BEGINNING

The Prairie Chicken Capital of the World, Rothsay, Minnesota, is my hometown. You might be surprised to learn that I've never actually seen a live prairie chicken. The closest I've come is the prairie chicken statue, built by my grandpa Art, which stands proudly along I-94.

Growing up in Rothsay was probably somewhat normal, somewhat typical. Both sets of grandparents lived in town, which I've come to appreciate as a huge blessing. We enjoyed summers at the family cabin at Lake Lida, played hours and hours of card games with relatives, and enjoyed the connectedness of a small school and small community.

Fun with my friends was my goal in those years, and we managed to have a lot of it while creating some great memories. Of course, in a small school, you can't help but be involved in lots of activities. Tried basketball (not my thing), tried track (not a runner), tried acting in a drama (was cast as a boy while I was in that awkward, low-confidence stage; that scarred me and halted my drama endeavors for years), played the saxophone (because we were supposed to be in band), competed in speech (but didn't see it impacting my future), was a cheerleader (I still am in many ways), and found that I had some talent on the volleyball court (THAT was fun).

You would think that I had too much going on to get into trouble. Unfortunately, that was not the case, and I didn't make it through my teenage years unscathed. I put my parents through a lot of frustration … and now that I'm a parent of teens, I really get it. My parents had practice with my older brother as he bent the rules, but I was equally, or perhaps more, rebellious.

The typical teenager thinks in terms of a 24 hour decision-making window, and I was no different. How will this decision right now impact me in the next 24 hours? That was how much thought I put into my stupid choices and even my future.

HOW *NOT* TO CHOOSE A COLLEGE MAJOR

I decided to go to college because that was pretty typical and that's what most of my friends were doing. I chose to major in interior design not because it was my passion, but because my brother's friend, Julie, majored in interior design. Julie was (and still is) pretty, sophisticated, and stylish. So, it made perfect sense in my teenage brain that if I wanted to be pretty, sophisticated, and stylish, I, too, should major in interior design.

Needless to say, that major didn't stick. I eventually realized that I wasn't particularly gifted in that field and certainly wasn't passionate about it.

Then I tried a graphic design focus, but that didn't stick either. So I took some general business classes and gradually I found myself working more during the day and going to school only at night. Eventually I ended up with a B.S. in Management from Minnesota State University, Moorhead. Get this – I even got halfway through a Master's Degree – not because I had a burning desire to get that degree, but because it seemed like a logical next step. Yep, I only got halfway through it because I was juggling a full-time job, marriage, and a baby and decided I didn't want it badly enough.

A CAREER BY DEFAULT

My 16-year human resource career certainly wasn't by design, either. After just a few years in my first real job, a co-worker said,

You're a people person, you should apply for the personnel job!

At that point I was an office assistant during the day and working toward a business degree part-time in the evenings. The traditional college path hadn't lasted long when my supervisor told me they were happy to have me for as many hours a week as I could manage. I loved my job and my co-workers; it only made sense to work more and to go school less.

"If you don't care where you're going, any road will get you there. "

- Lewis Carroll

So, this "people person" got the HR job and realized very quickly that it involved way more than being a "people person." Suddenly, I was administering payroll and benefits for hundreds of employees in a multi-state region. I had no clue what I was doing. I didn't understand taxes, let alone a flex plan, 401k plan, or FMLA. With trial by fire, you just do what you need to and find resources along the way. The owner of our payroll vendor spent countless hours helping me through the nitty-gritty of multi-state payroll. (That is the ONLY way everyone got paid correctly and on time in those early days with me running that show.) My contact at the placement agency, who had found me the job in the first place, connected me to the local HR association.

I didn't sign up for the 401k because I didn't think I could run that far.

That filled a critical gap – great connections, wonderful resources, study groups for the PHR and SPHR (yep, I eventually became certified with both designations). Thankfully, I acquired the knowledge and, over time, the experience to do the job well. All was good.

WHY CAN'T THINGS JUST STAY THE SAME?

The president of the company, my supervisor, was an amazing leader. He was a people person, the face of the organization, a great leader, and a great listener. All was good. I really thought I would work there forever. *Then, the inevitable happened; change.* Our wonderful company president announced his retirement and was replaced by someone with a completely different leadership style. I had been there nearly ten years and loved the company, but I wondered if I could handle the change. Change is an inevitable part of life, so I knew I needed to deal with it. I tried. I did. But when leadership changes and you no longer feel aligned with decisions, well, then, you've gotta do what you've gotta do.

> *"People join organizations; they leave managers."*
>
> *- Bill Hybels*

I know this shouldn't bring a smile to my face, but it still does. When I turned in my resignation, the new company leader was pretty surprised. He assumed I had another job (like most normal people would) so he asked where I was going. I chose my words carefully, and said, "I don't have another job; I just need to leave." Yes, I still feel a sense of satisfaction when I think about that.

After a few months of dabbling in temp jobs, enjoying more relaxed time with Steve and Alyssa, and organizing closets (okay, that's a lie; I didn't organize any closets), I accepted a job as the human resource director for a fairly large accounting firm. Before I accepted that position, I had my own uneducated opinion of what life at an accounting firm might look like: slow moving, stuffy, and perhaps a bit boring. Once I got to know the corporate team during the interview process, my perspective changed completely. This firm had aggressive plans for growth and was full of talented people working to create a wonderful culture. I took a big step into another unknown and took the job. The next few years were ripe with mergers, acquisitions of new business lines, de-mergers, and implementation of a complex performance management system. Bottom line = lots going on.

Personally, life was full at home as well; two little girls and a husband who had quit his job to start a business. The end of day involved a rush to pick up the girls before daycare closed, make a quick meal, play with the girls, do baths, reading and the bedtime routine, then it was time to open up the briefcase and tackle the pile of work that I didn't accomplish during the day. Most days included more chaos than calm. (Oh, yes, the fact that you're nodding tells me you can relate.)

Every once in a while I would see a glimmer of light at the end of the tunnel. Maybe relief was in sight? Nope. *That light at the end of the tunnel was just another train barreling down the tracks.* I felt so out of control – at one point, I was on the phone with a friend who was just as frazzled. The sad truth that I admitted to her that night was that if I were to get into a car accident and end up in the hospital, it would be a welcome break.

Looking back now, that is appalling! *A car accident would be a welcome break from the stress of life?*

It took me a little while, and a lot of frustration, to make a decision to do something different. I demoted myself to a part-time role (part-time being 30 + hours a week) and helped hire my new boss to take my former role. It was exactly what I needed. With the new HR director at the helm, work was fun again. My boss was one of the best leaders I've ever worked with; visionary, caring, honest, humble, and the list goes on. We were building a strong department and structuring for more growth. I must say I was pretty comfortable. Less pressure, less work, more peace.

> *"For fast acting relief, try slowing down."*
>
> *- Lily Tomlin*

Me = happy camper.

Me = comfortable.

All was good. If that had lasted, I may never have left that job.

PERSONAL UPHEAVAL

When the phone rang early that morning in July 2005, I knew it was bad news, but I didn't know what. Steve's face and his tone told me something terrible had happened. When he hung up the phone and told me that my dad had died, it didn't make any sense. My dad was a healthy, vibrant 60 year-old. And now he was gone. He had fallen during the night in the home he had built, the home in which I'd grown up.

When we imagined how dad would leave this earth, we envisioned a blaze of glory. He loved fast cars, boats, and his Harley-Davidson. But this? This didn't make any sense. I couldn't figure out why he had been taken from us at such a relatively young age and why he wouldn't be able to see his grandkids grow up.

I started searching for understanding. I prayed. I journaled. I started reflecting on what had transpired those weeks leading up to his death. One day we were at the lake, the girls were playing with their cousins, and my dad, Steve and I were just hanging out on the pontoon. I had my nose buried in a book, purposefully ignoring their conversation, because dad was talking about how he wanted us to celebrate his life when he died rather than mourn his death. I felt like that was such a morbid conversation and couldn't imagine dealing with that for years, so I buried my nose further in my book.

Another weekend in June, we were enjoying wine and conversation on the porch with our lake neighbors. My dad became a bit nostalgic. He shared the three times in his life he had been scared:

When he was in a car accident in the 80s and nearly died

When our daughter, Tara, one-and-a-half at the time, fell headfirst down a rocky hill at the lake and made everyone's heart stop

When my niece, Edyn, was critically ill in the hospital with the flu

It was an unforgettable conversation and a memorable evening, because it caused each of us to pause and really appreciate life and family.

Just days before he died, we celebrated Father's Day at the lake. Right before everyone departed, we remembered to take a photo of all the grandkids with their grandpa Tom. Now we have a treasured photo capturing the memories of that day.

All the events precipitating his death gave me a bit of comfort. It was as if he knew his time on earth was coming to an end. Over the weeks and months that followed, I attempted to find more meaning in his life, his legacy, and the lessons I could learn from it. *What I discovered was very enlightening.*

MY DAD'S LEGACY

My dad's resume must have been twenty pages long, no kidding. After nearly getting kicked out of college, he buckled down and earned a teaching degree. He taught and coached for several years. But that wasn't his lifelong career. He was a trailer salesman; he co-owned the local pool hall and truck stop; he became an insurance agent and eventually a district manager for that company; he became a huge advocate for education (even honored as one of the 1993 American Heroes in Education by the Reader's Digest Association) and helped create a student-run store; and, most surprising to us, he worked for a computer networking company and was able travel around the world as a trainer. We're still not sure how he got that job since he didn't even know how to operate a VCR! *If you are too young to know what a VCR is, Google it.*

From stepping back and looking at his life, my dad's path taught me that he followed his passions and had fun in the process. When he got out of the insurance industry after several years and much success, I recall him saying that he needed to leave because he wasn't having fun anymore. He wasn't worried about looking

> *"Your work is going to fill a large part of your life, and the only way to be truly satisfied is to do what you believe is great work. And the only way to do great work is to love what you do."*
>
> *- Steve Jobs*

like a job-hopper. He wasn't worried about what other people thought. He pursued his passions, enjoyed what he did, and made a huge impact on many others in his life. To me, that's a pretty cool legacy to leave.

This was what I needed to know at just the right time. As I was learning this and understanding the truth of his journey, I was contemplating what was in store for my future. His path played a big role in my decision to figure out what my passions were and to start pursuing them.

ON THE VERGE

Remember how I had been pretty comfortable in my job? Well, that didn't last. Two things happened. First, the legacy my dad left had really started to sink in, and I had this feeling that there was more ... I wasn't sure what, but I had this feeling. I was getting stronger in my faith, reading personal development books and attending workshops to work on "me." It felt like I was on the verge ... of something.

Secondly, my wonderful boss got offered a lucrative position at another organization and resigned. The timing of his departure was interesting, because the reporting relationships in our corporate office were changing. Because of this, the company leaders were hesitant to hire a new HR director until the structure was solidified. Understandable. In the meantime, I was named interim HR director and back in the saddle of a job I really didn't want. This "interim" role ultimately lasted over a year (sigh).

In the meantime, things were no longer comfortable.

My new boss, albeit a temporary boss, and I did not see eye to eye. At all. I felt like I had a blinking sign on my forehead that said "I'm getting fired any day, just not sure which day." In a conversation with him, I told him I was surprised he hadn't fired me yet. His response? "I'm surprised you haven't quit yet." In the words of comedian Bill Engvall, there's your sign. That was it. After nineteen years in the corporate world, I was burnt out and in need of a change. It was the push I needed to explore the next step, figure out how to be more passionate about what I was doing every

Sometimes things have to get really uncomfortable so you get that push to take the next step.

day, and make a difference in the world. Even if that meant I had to leave a perfectly good job with a nice steady paycheck and benefits.

TAKING A RISK

At the encouragement of my husband, I started contemplating self-employment. Steve had started a few different businesses and loved being his own boss, so he wanted the same for me. As we brainstormed and researched, we came across a coaching franchise and it resonated with me 100%. Coaching people to help them be more successful? Yes, I knew that was a fit. We traveled to the franchise site visit to further evaluate whether or not this was the right move. When we got back we had a postcard in the mail from our church. We had never received a mailing like this from them before.

"Every week we take time to pray for the members of our church. This week we are praying for your family."

Coincidence? No such thing. The next week, I gave my notice at work and we bought the franchise. It was the right fit at the right time and equipped me with resources to be off and running pretty quickly.

BURIED DREAMS

The year was 2009; I had been coaching others and wanted to keep learning and growing personally, so I enrolled in a "Goal Achiever" class. One of our weekly assignments was to write 100 goals. Things we wanted to be, do, or have. 100 goals? I had goals, but 100 of them?

Determined to follow through, I tackled the homework. I reflected, I dreamt, I wrote. Whoa. Something caught my eye.

At goal #33, I wrote "Become a keynote speaker." This caused me to pause. This was news to me, or so I thought.

Then a distinct memory popped into my mind.

I flashed back to 1992 when I had attended my first business conference sponsored by the North Dakota Human Resources Association. The speaker was engaging, dynamic and pretty much had me at hello. I vividly recall this thought popping into my mind as she spoke:

"I would love to do what she does."

And that was followed up by a second thought:

"But I could never do that."

Guess what I did? I dismissed that dream. I buried that dream! I buried it so deeply, under layers of doubt and limiting beliefs, that over time, I forgot I had that dream.

For me to remember that dream is another mini-miracle. My family knows how horrible my memory is, so for me to distinctly remember something from that many years ago was astonishing.

When I "rediscovered" that dream in 2009, let's be real: I had no idea *HOW* to go about it, but I just knew enough to take a step in that direction. So I purchased an audio book about public speaking and started listening and learning.

Pivotal moments can be positive or negative, and either way, they shape us.

The following week I shared this revelation with the small group of eight new friends. Here's where it gets even more interesting. One member of the group asked if I was serious about becoming a speaker. I told her I thought so – it felt like a nudge in a direction I needed to go. She proceeded to tell me she had purchased a package of seminars – one of the upcoming sessions was a Train-the-Trainer weeklong program. She wasn't interested in attending so it was her gift to me if I wanted to attend.

Free.

A gift.

I just needed to get myself to Los Angeles and pay for lodging. WOW! What an opportunity! Thank you, and yes, count me in! What are the odds of that?

The timing was perfect. There were great rates from Fargo to L.A. on specific days through Allegiant Air and they coincided with the training dates. Preparations were underway and was I excited! On the day of departure, I arrived to check in forty-four minutes before my flight.

Cool things happen. Sometimes it seems like coincidence. When I shared one of the mini-miracles with a friend, I said, "How cool is that? What are the odds of that happening?" Dennis replied, "With God, the odds are 100%." Profound. It's all part of the plan.

Two things to note here:

> *Minutes matter in my life. I try to make the most of each – so yes, it was forty-four minutes before departure.*

> *We're talking the Fargo airport, not O'Hare, so that timing is generally do-able.*

Imagine my surprise to arrive at check-in and see a sign that stated: "Check-in Closed: All guests must be checked in 45 minutes prior to departure." The service agent was shuffling papers behind the sign. A line was quickly forming behind me, six people deep. The service agent assured me and the others in line that the sign was accurate and we weren't getting on that flight. No refunds.

Maybe there was no way I could get on that flight, but there was no way I was missing the training. My budget was extremely tight (the year was 2009, anyone recall a recession?) and I had a decision to make. How badly did I want this? What was I willing to do to get there? I hustled to the United Airlines counter, was helped immediately, and $400 later, had another ticket to L.A. (And, yes, the training was amazing and just what I needed.)

Don't bury your dreams!

The world needs you and YOUR dreams!

Shortly after my trip to L.A., I booked my first keynote for an audience of 400. Even though it was my dream, it was daunting at the time. It was booked out nine months, so there was plenty of time for me to start panicking well in advance. As I was seeking advice from a friend who is also an inspirational speaker, she assured me I shouldn't be nervous; it's not about me - it's about the message I have to share that the audience needs to hear. I slept peacefully through the night again after hearing those words of wisdom.

Allowing My Kids to Dream

When our daughter, Alyssa, was ten, she discovered she really enjoyed acting. She was having fun with Missoula Children's Theatre, Fargo Moorhead Community Theatre, and porch plays at the lake under her direction. With her newly discovered passion, she dropped her plans to work in the medical field and decided to pursue acting. The conversation went something like this:

> *"Mom, I know what I wanna be when I grow up. I really want to be an actor."*

> *"That's great, honey – there are lots of fun ways to get involved in acting locally – The Fargo-Moorhead Community Theatre, Trollwood Performing Arts School, school plays..."*

> *"Well that's all fine, but I really want to be in movies, so I'm going to need an agent."*

She's ten ... living in Fargo, North Dakota ... her biggest role so far was a dwarf and she thinks she needs an agent?

As soon as those thoughts were popping into my mind, I recognized that I needed to challenge those thoughts. It doesn't matter where we live or what we think we are bound by; all that is possible for anyone is possible for us.

Well, here's where it got a little strange; I kept

> *"Don't tell me the sky's the limit when there are footprints on the moon."*
>
> *- Paul Brandt*

running into a lady who I eventually discovered was a talent agent for local models and actors. After our third encounter, I mentioned my daughter and her dreams, and the agent rolled her eyes with that look like "*tell me about it - every preteen wants those opportunities.*" Even so, she told me to bring Alyssa to an open call. Well, that open call led to four years of Alyssa pursuing that dream! She had some pretty amazing experiences, including multiple trips to Chicago and L.A. She was in TV commercials, prints ads, and even was chosen to emcee an event at age thirteen.

During her last trip to L.A., Alyssa spent nearly four weeks there. She was told she had great potential, and while there were no guarantees, we were advised to move to L.A. so she could fully devote the time and energy to her acting career.

At this point, Alyssa was a very social high school freshman – her friends were her world. What was she willing to sacrifice to pursue that dream? What were we (Steve and I) willing to give up? Steve and I weren't sure, but we decided to figure it out as we needed to. Guess what she decided? Not yet. Maybe someday, but not yet.

She has returned to her original plan to pursue a degree in the medical field.

Do we have any regrets? Absolutely none. The experiences gained and the lessons learned were invaluable. At a young age, she explored and took steps toward a dream. That, my friends, is more than many people do in a lifetime.

What about our daughter Tara? She has a passion for saving our environment, she has a soft spot in her heart for animals in need of rescue, and she's a dedicated athlete. Beyond that, her biggest dream is to never again be embarrassed by her mother. *Everything is possible but I'm not sure about that last point.*

GETTING MORE INTENTIONAL

Over time, I started getting more intentional with my business and my life. After studying and researching what makes successful people tick, I realized that mindset was one of the keys.

I realized that my mindset was critical to my happiness and success.

And, I discovered that mastering my mindset had to be an intentional part of my day, every day. I also realized that what was becoming more apparent to me was not necessarily apparent to others. And, if it was apparent, it wasn't practiced.

I intentionally began calling myself a mindset coach and conducting workshops to help people master their mindsets. And, of course, mastering your mindset must be followed by action and accountability! During this time, I started feeling more present in my life and the wonderful people in it.

After five years of being self-employed, I was gaining clarity about my passions, my strengths, and my purpose. Maybe for some people it comes clearly, quickly, and easily, but for me it has been a gradual refining process. I decided to rebrand my business and disengage from the franchise. The future was, as always, a bit unknown, yet it felt like the right decision. Later that month, I got a text from a friend insisting I attend an event that evening. According to my friend, "Scott Shickler, the mindset guy, is in Fargo and you have to go!" Yes, I did have to go; that night changed my life.

Just for today, get intentional about your mindset. (Then do it tomorrow, too.)

Scott Shickler, co-author of *The 7 Mindsets to Live Your Ultimate Life*, introduced The 7 Mindsets to me, my family, and a few hundred others that night. These are the mindsets that have been proven to lead to happiness and success. Scott's team in Atlanta, Georgia, had initiated a multi-year, multi-million dollar research project to determine what sets the happy and successful people apart from the rest. For me, that evening was a "hand meet glove" experience. I knew mindset mattered, but I hadn't invested millions of dollars or thousands of hours to prove it. And, I realized, I didn't have all the pieces to the mindset puzzle. The 7 Mindsets provided the rest of the puzzle pieces.

"Without the right mindset, skill loses its impact."

- Scott Shickler

Throughout the time I've been self-employed, I've explored a lot of open doors. Sometimes the open door was just the right thing at the right time, and sometimes the open door was not necessarily worth exploring further. You'll never know unless you explore the option.

I knew I wanted *needed* to be involved with The 7 Mindsets so I reached out to everyone I knew who was involved with that event. A few days later I had a conference call with Scott Shickler; shortly after that a face-to-face meeting. Our conversations led me to become a certified coach and speaker for The 7 Mindsets so I could share this mindset revolution with others.

The beauty of teaching and training is that you

get multiple opportunities to have the message sink in since you are constantly reading, learning, and sharing. The more I share the mindsets, the more I embrace the mindsets, the better the results. Yet, as you'll see, it definitely doesn't mean I've got it all figured out.

LETTING GO OF MY PLAN

It's so cool when a plan falls into place. It's just pretty rare that it happens that way!

It was an unexpected honor and amazing opportunity when I got invited to be on a national speaking team. This, I figured, was just what I needed to build my reputation, credibility, and visibility. There was excitement with that, and much to be done – create a press release, update my bio, update my profile on my website, social media, partner sites, etc. The national speaking team began getting together for Skype calls on a regular basis to keep connected and inspire each other.

Meanwhile, I was also working with a client to assist with a new business venture. It was a 30+ hour a week commitment for one year. Between that big client commitment, my other clients, family time, volunteering, and social life, well, that didn't leave a lot of extra time.

More and more, I found myself missing the

speaking team meetings due to other conflicts.

Right around this time, I was asked to speak at a faith-based luncheon a few months down the road. The specific topic was up to me to choose, and I was challenged by a friend to let go of what I want to talk about and embrace whatever it was that God wanted me to share. A group of prayer warriors were praying that by November 14, 2013, I would be guided to share what God wanted me to share.

Little did I know I should have asked God for an earlier deadline!

In the days and weeks approaching the event date, I wasn't hearing or feeling any direction. It would have been easy to put together a short talk based on mastering your mindset by faith or letting go and letting God, but I held fast and was determined to see what God would do.

"Failures, repeated failures, are finger posts on the road to achievement. One fails forward toward success."

- C. S. Lewis

On the morning of the event, guess what? I still had no clear guidance on what direction to take. My talk was at noon ... still a few hours to ask, pray, listen. At 10 a.m. I had a brief phone call with the leader of the national speaking team. We talked about how I hadn't been very connected to the rest of the team. And then, boom, I was kicked off the island (okay, just the team, but I can relate to what a Survivor contestant feels like). The team leader was kind and gentle, but the end result was that this team was not the right fit for me at this time. And, I had to admit that I agreed. As we were on the phone, I was absentmindedly writing notes and I wrote this ...

Every step creates momentum

I *knew* this was okay. It was a step I had taken, and it didn't work out. I *knew* that when one door closed, another would open. Knowing this though, didn't stop the tears. My ego was bruised. I was no longer part of the team. That part of me that likes to belong (a big part of me) felt excluded. And, then ...

Then I realized THIS is what God wanted me to share at the luncheon!

Are you kidding??

It was crystal clear. God had finally given me the direction I needed at 10:20 a.m. and I would have the microphone at noon. I needed to share this story, even as fresh and potentially painful as it was. I prayed and I talked to myself a lot in that short time period. And, I even got myself to the point of acceptance. This was all part of God's plan. I could label it as good or bad, but neither would matter. It was just part of His plan! There was freedom in knowing that.

There was also beauty in the answered prayer. I've come to realize that God often speaks to me through other people. Now I'm even more aware of this. And I'm learning it would be wise for me to ask God to share His guidance with me a little earlier in the process as I prepare for future events so I can eliminate the last-minute panic.

Sharing this message hit home with the audience at the luncheon. I even joked about how now I needed to further bruise my ego and undo all the profiles and online references to the speaking team. One person told me it was exactly what he needed to hear that day. Things were not going according to his plan and he had been hanging on tightly to that plan. He realized it was time to let go of what he couldn't control and surrender to "His plan."

This reminds me of a parable I've heard in different forms over the years:

A farmer bought a horse and not long after, it ran away. A neighbor said, "That's bad news." The farmer replied, "Good news, bad news, who knows?"

The horse came back and brought another horse with him. Good news, you might say.

The farmer gave the second horse to his son, who rode it, was thrown, and badly broke his leg.

"So sorry for your bad news," said the neighbor. "Good news, bad news, who knows?" the farmer replied.

The following week, every able-bodied young man was called to fight in a war. The farmer's son was spared. Good news!

We can label our circumstances as good or bad at the time, and later have a change of heart based on new information and different conditions.

Good news, bad news, who knows?!

At that same monthly luncheon at which I spoke, I connected with some great people from Life 97.9, a local Christian radio station. They encouraged me to apply for a job as a part-time morning co-host, from 6-9 a.m. weekdays. My schedule was *overflowingly full* at the time, with 30+ hours a week dedicated to one client, so I knew there was no way I could fit it in, even on a part-time basis. Furthermore, I could *never* be on the radio: I don't keep up with world events, I'm not spontaneously clever nor have I ever been a role model for making it to work on time. And this involved being awake and on air at 6 a.m.?

Ha! That was definitely not in my future. In fact, I declined the invitation to apply and referred them to a friend.

At the next luncheon, we talked again and they invited me to the radio station for monthly interviews to share The 7 Mindsets from a faith basis. That seemed like a great opportunity to introduce the mindsets to more people, so I became a monthly guest on Life 97.9.

POWER BEHIND PASSION AND PURPOSE

Two months later, we focused on Mindset #2, Passion First, and I shared some insights on air. Pursuing your passions is ultimately what this mindset is about. However, we often leave passion out of the equation when making decisions about our future and our career.

Most of us base employment decisions on the paycheck and the perks instead of the passion.

That doesn't necessarily lead to happiness, success, or fulfillment in life. After sharing the Passion First mindset on air, we received an email from someone who took the message to heart and opened up her mind to new possibilities.

"You were born by His purpose and for His purpose."

- Rick Warren

Here's what she shared in her email:

"Because of that conversation on air I have switched my educational goals. I was in my 2nd semester of Business Administration and I have made the switch to social work. My goal is to work with teenage girls or young moms in crisis situations. I was sexually assaulted as a young teen, became pregnant, and now have a wonderful 8 year old. I also had a child at the age of 18 and chose adoption (she's now 5 and it's a wonderful choice - open adoption!). I want to use my life to help others get through their dark times. The message that day really hit me. It made me realize I was not doing what God put me on earth to do. I'm so excited for my educational path. I am just getting started and I have a long way to go. But I know with God all things are possible!!"

Wow. When I went on air to share how much your mindset matters, I really thought it would be great awareness for people. Little did I know that a short segment could change the course of a person's life. We all ask ourselves the question, "Does what I do matter?" It does.

Every day we are making an impact.

One of my prayers at this time was to broaden my reach. In order to make a positive and profound difference in the world, I felt called to reach more people. And, of course, I wanted to have my cake and eat it, too; I wanted to broaden my reach in a way that didn't take me away from home too much. Our daughters were teenagers and I wanted to be home as much as I could since these years were going so fast.

Flash forward a few months when my 30+ hour a week contract ended with that client – once again my schedule had a bit more flexibility. The team at Life 97.9 had kept the conversations going about joining them part-time. It finally dawned on me that this was an answered prayer to broaden my reach. A radio station, less than five minutes from my house, with the ability to impact thousands. That was an unexpected blessing. God is good!

"Nothing is as important as passion. No matter what you do with your life, be passionate."

- Jon Bon Jovi

How could I be expected to get up early and be on air Monday through Friday when I used to have a tough time getting to work by 8?

The answer lies in passion and purpose.

And, feeling aligned with the mission and the ministry provided by the station. There's also the fact that the show will go on with or without you, so you better show up. Never say never. Even I can speak somewhat coherently before the sun is up!

Meanwhile, Steve pursues his passions

My husband, Steve, and I actually worked together in that very first job I had – the job where I started my human resource career. We didn't technically meet there, though. How we met is a whole different story. (It involves me living with his ex-fiancé but, to be clear, I was not the cause of their breakup – they did that all on their own.)

When I was going through files in our home office when we were newly married, I found some old files from a job he held in college at a lawn care company. My temptation was to get rid of the files, but Steve told me he always wanted to own a lawn care company, so he wanted to hang on to those files (and that dream).

Sure enough, that dream took shape a few years later as he started his business. When he quit his job to run his business full-time, I wouldn't say I was 100% supportive; I hadn't had visions of him owning a seasonal business that involved a fair amount of risk. In spite of my hesitation, he ran a successful lawn care business for sixteen years. Also during that time he became a volunteer for the local fire and rescue team (also a dream of his) and was hired to coach a high school football team (yet another dream).

In the fall of 2014 as the two of us headed out for

a mountain getaway, Steve told me he was ready for a change. He was considering getting out of the lawn care business and trying something new. He had held his commercial real estate license for three years and wanted to focus more on that business. On that trip, we decided to move forward and see if anyone was interested in buying the lawn care business.

Much to my surprise, we found an interested party quite quickly. I had to set my hesitation aside and come to terms with risk-taking again. The lawn care business was seasonal; it was tough to find good help and the weather didn't always cooperate, but at least it was a known quantity. Now, we were going to take another risk in the name of pursuing passions.

"The biggest risk is not taking any risk."

- Mark Zuckerberg

Feel the fear and take the next step in spite of it.

Sure enough, in a matter of months, his lawn care business (his baby) was sold and Steve's focus turned to commercial real estate. The new owners of the lawn care business decided not to offer snow removal, so we rebranded and launched a new snow removal company. Now he is devoted to commercial real estate full-time and running a snow removal company part-time.

Will there be more risks in our future? Oh, I can almost guarantee it. I think I'll keep my seatbelt on for the fun!

LIFE WITH TEENAGERS

Since I'm at the radio station before anyone else is awake and I get home after they are on their way for the day, imagine my surprise when our daughter Tara tells me that she overslept, was almost late for school and it's my fault. Wait a minute – MY fault? Normally she's on her A game – she gets herself up and out the door after I'm gone and she's already at school by the time I get home. So, how on earth can this be MY fault? Here's what she said to me:

> "You know how you say garbage in, garbage out and you want me to listen to positive messages instead of the negative stuff that's out there?"

> "Yeah..."

> "Well I decided to start listening to Life 97.9 more and I even set my alarm to that station. And, here's the deal, I'm so used to TUNING YOU OUT so that's what I did. I overslept. So, you see, it's all your fault."

The great thing is that part of my message is sinking in with my teenagers, but I guess we still need a bit of work on accountability. Isn't that true for all of us?

One day, Steve and I were enjoying a beautiful summer morning on the deck at the lake. We watched as our adorable four-year-old neighbor skipped and sang as she helped her grandma pick up branches in the yard to add to the fire pit. She reminded us so much of our daughters at that age … talkative, easy-going, and easily entertained. As I sipped my coffee, I found myself lamenting the fact that our teenage daughters, at that time 17 and 14, were not always talkative, easy-going, or easily entertained. Oh, how I longed for days past when I could say, "Let's go to the park!" and they would be thrilled beyond measure and ready to go before I could blink. Now, I could say "Let's go to the mall!" and even that would be met with resistance and certain criteria (could their friends come, how much money would I give them, what stores would we go to, and so on).

Embrace and appreciate each stage your kids are in; the stages pass quickly.

Then there was the stark reality that most days they no longer thought I was cool. In their younger days, I could goof around, tease them and be silly, and they obviously adored me. Now, most attempts at fun and craziness are met with a variety of responses from cringing to eye-rolling. Simply put, it's a transition from adoration to agitation.

Just days after I had these thoughts, I was preparing to speak about embracing an "attitude of gratitude" mindset. It dawned on me on that as much as I focused on that mindset and practiced it in many areas of life, I was falling short as a parent of teens. I was wishing for days gone by and not fully appreciating the blessings right in front of me. While our daughters may not always be talkative, easy-going, or easily entertained, they had grown up to be smart, independent, confident, and not afraid to express their thoughts. THAT is a lot to be grateful for! I realized I needed to get back to being grateful for what was right in front of me. With that realization, I made an intentional effort to appreciate their independence and cut them a little slack for being, well, teenagers.

A few weeks later, we took a family vacation.

The four of us.

In a car.

For several hours.

I was equipped with my attitude of gratitude.

What unfolded in the next few days was, in my eyes, a mini-miracle. We all got along better than we normally do on a car trip; it was easy and relaxing. In fact, at one point, the girls were in the backseat singing as they recalled lyrics from nursery rhymes sung in grandma's car. Rather than commenting on it and risking agitation, I silently said a prayer of thanks for little moments such as these. The singing continued. *Internal happy dance!*

Most of us can recall our teenage years and remember the emotional roller coaster. It's like walking a tightrope where you crave your freedom but are wary of the independence and all it entails. It's not an easy time. Most of us would agree that the challenges teens face now are multiplied when compared to what other generations faced.

"Don't let yourself be so concerned with raising a good kid that you forget you already have one."

- Glennon Melton

Knowing they are facing overwhelming emotions and situations doesn't give them free reign for disrespect. We can help them mature by having compassion, listening when they are ready to talk, and providing a safe haven for them.

Speaking of safe havens – that was another thing we've had to come to terms with. We found that

"Dear parents, Knocking while you open the door to my room kinda defeats the purpose of knocking."

- Teenagers

our teens wanted to be holed up in their rooms for extended periods of time. Teens need their space and it's okay to give it to them, as long as it's not evidence of a more significant withdrawal issue. According to child psychologist, Dr. Peter Marshall, "privacy is important for teens partly because they need to separate. It's tempting to think that they're just goofing off, but they spend a large part of their time just thinking about things, trying to figure out who they are, who they want to become. There's a lot of work for them to do, and they need some space to do it."*

It wasn't too long ago that Tara, following in the footsteps of Alyssa at the same age, began spending more and more time in her room. One Saturday she was home and very content to be in her room. So content, in fact, she probably would have been in there all day. Recognizing this, I gave her a three-hour time limit to be in her room. I set a reminder on my phone so I would be sure to follow through (something I've not always excelled at). As the deadline approached, nearly to the minute, I heard the creaking of her door and then a bit of commotion. Further

Source: The Parent Report www.theparentreport.com/2013/04/why-teenagers-need-privacy

investigation indicated she was getting settled *in the hallway* outside of her bedroom with her bean bag, blanket, and book! (Well, I guess she met the technical requirements of the rule...)

We've all heard it before – "the time goes fast – before you know it, they'll be graduating" – we've heard this and we think we understand but we don't really take it to heart. We get too caught up in the moments, the sleepless nights, the tantrums, the endless questions of "why," and the challenges of a full schedule. Everything is a stage, the stages will pass quickly, and someday we will wish we had these moments again (at least some of them). This holds true for the enjoyable stages and the not-so-enjoyable stages.

I'm constantly presented with opportunities to practice embracing an attitude of gratitude.

Like when my newly-licensed-to-drive daughter was backing my car out of the driveway. I was moving grandpa's vehicle so she could back out. Imagine my thoughts as I (too far away to do anything) could see the front end of my car scraping against a trailer that was also in the driveway! My first thought was not one of gratitude; in fact, I said some words that weren't very pleasant or uplifting. Thankfully, in a matter of minutes, I calmed down and gave her the "it's only a car" speech. And, shortly after, we were able to laugh about it.

As I considered what to be grateful for in this situation, here are a few thoughts that came to my mind:

We have not only one, but two daughters who are healthy and happy; some people don't.

Our daughters still have one of their grandpas around; some people don't.

We have cars to drive; some people don't.

Now my front fenders match; My car met a boulder (okay, a large rock on a boulevard) with the other fender a few months prior, so there's that.

No matter how old your kids are, know that where they are now is a stage and within each stage there is much to be grateful for.

As for me, maybe my kids just aren't letting on that they think I'm still cool. I believe I'll hold on to that thought and be grateful for them, no matter what.

AMAZINGLY EXHAUSTING

Living by default doesn't always require a lot of energy. Complacency definitely doesn't require a lot of energy. Living by design does require a lot of energy. In fact, it can be *amazingly exhausting*.

Some days contain tears of joy; some days contain tears of frustration; some days contain both.

Is it always exhilarating? No. Will you occasionally want to throw in the towel and give up? Yes. What's important is that you keep going.

Recently, a colleague (also a speaker and soon-to-be-author) and I connected on a Skype call to get to know each other better and were astounded to realize our challenges were so similar. There's such blessing in connecting with others who are on a similar path. Connections like that give me the energy and the courage to keep moving forward.

It's easy to start. Anyone can start. Persistence demands strength and courage.

AM I "THERE" YET?

I'm grateful that my story isn't finished yet, it's only this part of the book that's finished. To sum up my journey, by taking one step at a time and through the grace of God, I am blessed to do what I love. Speaking to audiences and coaching individuals and teams is how I can give the world the best version of myself.

Let's be clear that I know I'm not there yet.

I haven't arrived, and actually don't anticipate that I ever will while on this planet.

The more I know, the more I know I don't know.

I just hope if I'm blessed with another tomorrow, I will be better than I am today.

LESSONS I'VE LEARNED ON MY JOURNEY THAT CAN HELP YOU WITH YOURS

BACK TO THE BASICS: A FORMULA FOR SUCCESS

Acclaimed UCLA basketball coach John Wooden was known for teaching his new recruits something fundamental. The first order of business wasn't conditioning, it was instructing the new player how to put their socks and shoes on. Wrinkled socks could result in blisters; blisters could result in pain and an off-game. A poorly tied shoe could come untied and result in injury.

Some of the lessons we must re-learn (and put into practice) are the fundamentals. That's where we begin.

Years ago, I was introduced to Jack Canfield's book, *The Success Principles.* One of the principles that really resonated with me is a formula that is fundamental to living a life by design. Since I'm a bit numerically challenged, you can imagine my excitement when I came across this formula with letters:

$E + R = O$

   E = *events and experiences* that impact us, often outside of our control

   R = our *response* Notice that the R is not labeled as *reaction*; the distinction is significant. Reaction implies a knee-jerk reaction without any forethought. A response is intentional; you get to choose your response.

   O = the *outcome* of the situation

The variable we have control over in every situation is our response. Simple math concepts from that formula demonstrate that our response can change the outcome of the situation. It is both simple and profound; for any event or experience we face, we get to choose our response and that response influences the outcome.

Our responses are based on our choices in that moment and past experiences that have shaped us. That explains why two people can have completely different responses to the same situation.

This simple formula has been adopted by the Ohio State Buckeyes with results that caught the attention of The Wall Street Journal. WSJ Sports Reporter Ben Cohen shared how the team has undergone extensive training to help them respond in a positive way to almost every imaginable event. Rather than a knee-jerk reaction to an unexpected event, the team is choosing to respond in a way that positively influences the outcome.*

We *know* this, yet are we *doing* this?

MIND THE GAP: If you've been to the United Kingdom, you've heard this as you've boarded a train. It's a safety warning to remind us to pay attention to the gap between the station platform and the train door. A big challenge that we each face is that we are unaware of the gaps that exist in our lives. It's when we take time to reflect and evaluate that we identify the gaps and are then able to "mind the gap."

There can be a big gap between knowing and doing.

Our lives are a culmination of our responses to the situations

---

* Source: *The Power of Ohio State's Positive Thinking* by Ben Cohen, *Wall Street Journal*, April 13, 2015.

and people we encounter every day. In my experience, many of us highly educated, extremely capable adults don't take control of our responses and that, my friends, is reflected in our outcomes.

Ultimately, it boils down to this: Control what you can; let go of the rest!

"God, grant me the serenity to accept the things I cannot change, the courage to change the things I can and the wisdom to know the difference."

The Serenity Prayer

THE ILLUSION OF CONTROL

One of the fundamentals is to understand the illusion of control.

Control is an interesting phenomenon - we wish we could control others, we hate feeling out of control, and we fear being controlled by others. Think of how often we have had a good plan and then factors outside of our control threw everything off course. The plan is out the window, and we are disappointed and surprised because something came up to throw us off course! Should we be surprised? It almost seems like we should be more surprised when things *don't* come up to throw us off course.

It seems that the more uncertainty and insecurity we encounter, the more we try to assert our control, even if it's in vain. The "illusion of control" is an effect named by psychologist Ellen Langer. The premise is that we believe we can control, or at least influence, outcomes over which we truly have no influence.*

Consider this: does the strength of your throw while rolling dice impact the numbers you roll? Of course not! Langer's research, however, found that when gamblers rolled dice in the casinos, they tended to throw harder when they needed high numbers and they threw softer for low numbers. It sounds ridiculous, but it is true. This is a perfect example of how we highly intellectual human beings succumb to the illusion of control.

Another study revealed that the majority of drivers feel safer when they are driving a vehicle as opposed to being a passenger. That same majority are the ones at the wheel still having accidents. That brings back memories of my mom in the passenger seat when I was a new driver; she was bracing for dear life and wildly pressing the nonexistent brake pedal in front of her. *Now that I think about it, the last time I drove her car with her in the passenger seat was just a few weeks ago. She did the same thing then, too!* Ah, the illusion of control.

*Source: Langer, Ellen J. (1975), "The Illusion of Control", Journal of Personality and Social Psychology 32 (2): 311–328, doi:10.1037/0022-3514.32.2.311

FOCUS ON WHAT YOU CAN CONTROL

One way to regain control in an out-of-control world is to focus on what you can control. To do that, we need to get clear on what we can control and then commit to taking control of that. There is a great deal we can control, yet in many areas we are not stepping up and taking control! We're on autopilot, rushing for no reason, dishing out excuses for the choices we make, and blaming others for our results. It doesn't have to be that way. We have a choice.

What do we have control over? Think of the thousands of choices we make every day – the words we speak, what we eat, what we drink, whether or not we exercise, what we say yes to, what we say no to.

We also have choices over what we expose ourselves to.

Do you regularly expose yourself to brain food or would it be considered mind pollution?

This is about what you listen to, what you watch, what you read, who you surround yourself with, the thoughts you think.

Let's dive into each of these areas so we can really get a handle on this.

Your Dreams

Think back to when you were a kid. Do you remember those days when the world was full of possibilities and the sky wasn't even the limit? I remember those days. My friends and I could play house for hours using only our imagination and a few cherished props from grandma's closet.

When we were kids, it was as if we could look out the big window of life and picture the possibilities.

"There are only 3 colors, 10 digits and 7 notes; it's what we do with them that's important."

- Jim Rohn

Then, life happened and we experienced bumps in the road; rejection, failure, and disappointments. To keep ourselves safe, we lowered our dreams. Some of us lowered our dreams so much that we've simply given up dreaming. We've settled and perhaps we've even become complacent.

Remember that window full of possibilities? Eventually the shade starts to lower on our dreams and our view of the world. We no longer see possibilities, just a limited view of the world. Those are the moments where you wonder, "Is this it?"

What *were* your dreams? What *are* your dreams?

Have you buried any of your dreams because of those little voices in your head telling yourself you weren't worthy or capable?

"To give your passionate self to the world is the greatest gift you can give the world."

- Mark J. Lindquist

We were all created for a purpose. If you think your life purpose is to keep up with the Joneses, sport the latest fashions, or to have your home magazine-ready, so be it. Just please give this some thought. Why are you here? What matters to you? How can you make a difference in this world?

Your Choices

Having choices is a luxury, yet it can also be overwhelming. We are faced with thousands of choices every day. The choices we make today create the results we see tomorrow. Should I hit the snooze button or jump out of bed? Should I grab a pastry and a soda or make a healthier choice? How do I prioritize my activities? What tone do I use with my spouse and my kids? Do I need to pause before responding in frustration? Am I starting the day with a smile? (If you're happy, be sure to tell your face.)

What if we started being more intentional about our choices? Once you start living a life by design, you eliminate the guilt. Since your priorities and values guide your decisions, you'll be able to make sound decisions intentionally. You get to choose what's on your plate, both literally and figuratively.

We have endless choices for how to spend our time, our energy and our money. Choose wisely.

I recall a conversation at work when I was twenty-something and working full-time and going to college part-time. At that stage, of course, I thought I had the world all figured out. My co-worker, who was older and in a much different season of life, was talking about how he and his wife walked three miles a night, every night. I told him it must be nice to have time to do that! His response to me is one that I still remember: "Teresa, you and I both have the same 24 hours in a day; it's just a matter of how you choose to use them." I heard his reply and understood his reply, but I really didn't *get it* until much later in life.

Every choice, every decision we make every day has three possible outcomes:

Positive impact

Negative impact

Neutral impact

Those choices that impact us positively take a little more effort than those that impact us negatively. For instance, it's easy to skip the workout, but we know today's physical activity will have a long-term positive impact. Likewise, it's easier to overdo it on the brownies and eat half the pan than it is to refrain and enjoy a (yes, one) brownie.

Make choices not excuses.

Choices that impact us negatively will ultimately zap our energy, lead us down a path of self-sabotage and sidetrack us from living our best life.

Your Mindset

Consider a situation where things are not going very well at work. You're frustrated and it feels like nothing is going your way.

One choice: You continue on the negative spiral. They are all out to get you, this always happens to you and there is no hope for your current situation. You complain to all who will listen (and even those who don't) about how awful it is. You get home and take your frustrations out on your family. The result? Mountains of negativity, no hope, and probably a sleepless night.

A better option: You pause and intentionally refocus your mind. You take a few minutes to focus on everything in your life you are grateful for. You have a job; some people don't. You are probably getting paid fairly well; some people aren't. You have a safe environment in which to work; some people don't. Most of the time, you really enjoy what you do; some people don't. This will help your mind get to a better state. You'll look at the situation with a fresh perspective.

Same situation, different outcomes simply because of your mindset. Your mindset matters. Intentionally shifting your perspective about a situation can produce huge dividends right away. It's good for your well-being, your health, and your relationships.

Merriam-Webster defines mindset as "a particular way of thinking: a person's attitude or set of opinions about something." When we talk mindset, we are talking about challenging our current perspective to look at the situation in a new, more helpful way.

After years of studying habits and behaviors of successful people, I discovered that having the right mindset is critical to any field, any profession, any person, any age, and any stage.

This truth doesn't diminish the importance of skills, knowledge, education, or certifications. It just means that with the right mindset, you can make an even greater impact.

Think about the last time you had a day that didn't go so well – your skills were the same as the day before and the day after, yet it was your mindset that made the difference for how your day turned out. And, even while you were having that "bad" day, you probably knew that you weren't in a good place. First, it's critical to recognize that you're in a bad place, and then it's up to you to take steps to shift your mindset.

The Mindsets that Matter Most

After I had been learning how much our mindset matters and speaking on that subject, I was introduced to the work of The 7 Mindsets team. They had embarked on a quest to determine what sets the happy and successful people apart from the rest of the population. Their multi-year, multi-million dollar research study encompassed existing research, hundreds of books, hundreds of interviews and data from working with over 200,000 teens. What they discovered is that the world's happiest, most successful, most fulfilled people had in common was their mindset. And, there are 7 mindsets in particular they share. I'll share them as an overview here, and I encourage you to read The 7 Mindsets to Live Your Ultimate Life by Scott Shickler and Jeff Waller.

Mindset #1 Everything is Possible

Mindset #2 Passion First

Mindset #3 We are Connected

Mindset #4 100% Accountable

Mindset #5 Attitude of Gratitude

Mindset #6 Live to Give

Mindset #7 The Time is Now

At first glance, even without knowing more about The 7 Mindsets, you might nod and agree that, sure, that looks like an appropriate list that would define how the world's most successful people think. Knowing and agreeing are one thing; embracing those mindsets every day, in every situation? That's a whole 'nother level and that's the level we strive for.

As I mentioned earlier, the great news about mindset shifts is that the results are immediate. And for those of us (likely the entire population of our microwave society) who enjoy immediate gratification ... THAT is music to our earbuds.

Let me share an example. I had a request from a financial advisor to meet over coffee. This was in a season where I was coffee'd out – lots and lots of coffee meetings, some fruitful, others not so much. He extended the invitation to meet so we could each learn about each other's business. My first inclination was to say "no, thank you" since I thought this meeting wouldn't be very productive; he would be vying for my business and I was very happy with my financial advisor. I decided to switch my mindset, look forward to meeting someone new, and just be upfront with him about the fact that I was not a good prospect for him. So we met and had a great discussion that even involved a little brainstorming about how he could keep motivated in his field. Imagine my surprise when that meeting resulted in him signing up as a new coaching client.

Your mindset matters! Get intentional about mastering it!

Your Gratitude

Several years ago, a lunch speaker challenged the audience to be in a state of gratitude for one whole day. From the moment we woke up the next day, we were challenged to notice and appreciate all aspects of life (a comfortable bed, electricity, a hot shower, a new day dawning, the people around us) and embrace gratitude throughout the entire day. I've attempted this a few times, and while I can't say I've been able to keep my focus all day long (due to the ongoing challenge of bright, shiny objects), the new appreciation I have gained for blessings I previously took for granted has been pretty incredible.

There are numerous studies citing the health benefits of gratitude: it reduces stress, it increases our immunity, helps us sleep better, and enables us to better manage challenges that arise. Embracing a feeling of gratitude actually changes our physical state by increasing the level of endorphins in our body.*

Researchers in the field of positive psychology tell us that our brains perform 31% better in a positive state as opposed to a negative, neutral or stressed state.** One way to shift into a positive state immediately is by focusing on what you are grateful for. We can change our mood and become more productive immediately by choosing gratitude. It's simple, but not always easy.

Gratitude is the bridge from entitlement to blessing.

How can you become more grateful?

Start by noticing and being grateful for the things you may take for granted. Think of everything there is to be grateful for from the moment you wake up in the morning (shelter, a cozy bed,

* Sources: 2011 study published in Applied Psychology: Health and Well-Being, 2012 study published in Personality and Individual Differences. www.greatergood.berkeley.edu Robert A. Emmons, Ph.D.
**Source: The Happy Secret to Better Work, Shawn Achor, www.ted.com

electricity, running water). 783 million people don't have access to clean water while many of us complain that our shower takes too long to get warm.*

"Gratitude is the healthiest of all human emotions. The more you express gratitude for what you have, the more likely you will have even more to express gratitude for."

- Zig Ziglar

Start a gratitude journal. You can create a habit to be grateful by simply focusing your thoughts on what you are thankful for each and every day. There are apps for that (of course) or you may find it helpful to write (yes, pen and paper) what you are grateful for. Doing this every day will form the habit quickly, but if you fall off the wagon and forget to journal for a day or two, just start again when you think of it.

Become aware of all the blessings in your life that didn't appear initially as blessings. When times are good, it's easy to count your blessings. However, if you are going through a particularly tough time, this can be a challenge. But, if you consider how your situation could be worse, you might be able to find the good in the here and now. No one ever said life would be easy; we will serve ourselves well once we learn to be grateful in any situation.

*Source: www.unwater.org

Consider random acts of gratitude. Thank your co-workers and colleagues with a written note, send a card to let your customer know you appreciate their business, find opportunities to tell your spouse and kids thank you.

Seek out the good. Continually turn your attention from what's not going well to what is going well. If you look for the negative, you will find it. If you look for the positive, you will find it.

Embrace gratitude and make it a part of your routine. Eventually it will become a habit. It's good for your body, mind, and soul.

Far too often, we see evidence that we live in an age of entitlement. We operate under the assumption that we deserve the best, the latest, the greatest and nothing less.

When we choose gratitude, we pause to focus on what is in our life rather than what's missing from our life. Then, we express thanks for those blessings. It's not about being grateful only for what's going well; it's about being grateful in all circumstances.

Give thanks in all circumstances; for this is God's will for you in Christ Jesus.

1 Thessalonians 5:18

You may not be familiar with the name Horatio Spafford, but maybe you've heard the beautiful hymn he wrote, "It is Well

With My Soul." Here is a snapshot of his life and what he experienced prior to writing that song. His only son died from scarlet fever. Later he was financially ruined in the Great Chicago Fire. Shortly after that, as his wife and four daughters were traveling by ship to Europe, the ship sunk and only his wife survived. On his way to meet his grieving wife, he was inspired to write these words as his ship passed near where his daughters had died; "Whatever my lot, thou has taught me to know, it is well, it is well with my soul." Can you imagine the peace he must have known to be able to pen such impactful words at such a time of loss? Spafford truly knew what it meant to be grateful in any and all circumstances.

A word of caution for the attitude of gratitude. Occasionally I work with women who are truly victims and have escaped an abusive situation. First, please know I'm not advocating that anyone find the positives in an abusive situation and continue to tolerate abuse. The priority is to take control and get out of that situation as soon as possible. I also can assure you that I've met survivors of abuse who have gained strength from their trials to help them rise above and help others in similar situations.

Your Thoughts

It's been said that we have approximately 60,000 thoughts a day and at least 80% of those thoughts are negative.

Our thoughts can help us or hurt us. Our thoughts dictate our actions, which lead to our results. So if we can get better at controlling our thoughts, instead of our thoughts controlling us, we will get better results.

Our thoughts stem from our mindset or our perspective on the situation. If our mindset is that we expect the worst, rather than the best, we look for evidence that matches our expectation and our thoughts take shape around that.

"I knew I'd mess that up."

"That never works for me."

"I'll never lose weight."

"There aren't enough hours in the day."

Let's take that last thought and work through that. Most of us have been there. We get overwhelmed and feel like there's too much to do and not enough time to do it all. And that is probably true! Our get-to-do lists keep getting longer. Of course, prioritization will help, and we also need to reframe our thoughts about our available hours relative to our get-to-do list. Let's walk through an example of this.

Employ the 4 R's to Change Your Thoughts

Defeating thought: "There aren't enough hours in the day."

Recognize: The first step is to recognize the negative, defeating thought. *"Aha! I'm aware I had that negative thought!"*

Refuse: Next, refuse that thought. *"That's not an empowering thought. That thought has negative energy."*

Replace: Now, replace that thought with something more helpful. *"We all have the same 24 hours in a day; there are enough hours to accomplish what's most important."*

Repeat: Repeat your new phrase often (aloud or in your head, either will work). You might even find it helpful to write this on an index card next to your computer, or incorporate it into your passwords. Whatever you can do to cement it in your mind, do it.

Did you know? Thinking positively about aging helps you live longer.

Consider this as it relates to the power of your thoughts. A study published in Psychological Science Journal found that positive attitudes about aging can prolong life expectancy. And, on the flip side, negative attitudes about aging can diminish life expectancy. Becca R. Levy, PhD, of Yale University, and colleagues discovered that adults with positive attitudes about aging lived 7.5 years longer than their peers with negative attitudes. They concluded that "self-perceptions of aging had a greater impact on survival than did gender, socioeconomic status, loneliness and functional health."

Your Self-Talk

One specific facet of our thoughts is our self-talk. Sometimes, this self-talk is actually spoken out loud, giving it even more significance. Everyone has an inner dialogue – yes, we all talk to ourselves. If you're not convinced, start paying attention to your thoughts throughout the day. How many are directed at yourself and your capabilities or behaviors?

Since we're talking to ourselves anyway, shouldn't we have some control over what messages we are sending?

Suppose you've been trying to lose weight for years. Your inner voice says, *"I'm so overweight, I've tried 20 diets and none of them worked."* What if you changed that inner voice to say, *"I'm exercising more and eating healthier – each day I'm getting better and better."* And, then, follow up it up with action (i.e., exercising more, eating healthier, portion control.)

See if any of these inner dialogues are familiar to you:

"I'm not equipped to do this."

"I'll never amount to anything. Why am I even trying?"

"Everyone else has it together except me."

"I'm always running late."

"Why do I always leave it until the last minute?"

"Will I ever get it right?"

"I'm such a loser; nobody else would do anything as dumb as me."

Would you be upset if someone else talked to you like this? I would hope so. Then why would you allow your own little voices to continually berate you?

The first step to changing the way you talk to yourselfisawareness;payattentiontothethoughts you have, then work to change that internal dialogue to be more empowering and positive.

The Words You Speak

Words matter. Words have power. Words can build up or tear down. Your words impact your self-image, your confidence and greatly impact your relationships with others.

Spend some time just listening to conversations at work, at the store, at the gym. The overwhelming majority of conversations you'll hear are negative in nature, more focused on problems than solutions and focused on tearing others down.

Do an inventory today to see what words come out of your mouth throughout the day. How much is negative? How much do you complain? How often do you criticize others? Are you focusing on what you want or what you don't want?

If you are tired of the drama in your life, then quit talking about it, all the time, with everyone you encounter. It doesn't mean you shouldn't deal with it in an emotionally healthy way. It just means you don't give it any more energy than necessary.

No more grumbling, no more complaining. Could you go one full day without grumbling or complaining? How about three days, or a week? Think about this; just three days after God parted the Red Sea for Moses to lead the Israelites out of Egypt, the Israelites began grumbling and complaining. They had just experienced firsthand

"Any fool can criticize, complain and condemn – and most fools do. But it takes character and self-control to be understanding and forgiving."

- Dale Carnegie

God performing one of the most amazing miracles ever recorded and within days they resorted to whining and complaining. I'd like to think I would have behaved differently, but perhaps that's giving me a little too much credit.

It's easy to complain. It takes discipline to refrain.

It's easy to whine and complain and proclaim life's inconveniences and minor injustices. Many people are fueled by those conversations. Even if we know it's not right, it's easy to fall into complaining mode. *(Sometimes it's way too easy.)* It's much more difficult to refrain, bite your tongue, and live by the old adage, "if you can't say anything nice, then don't say anything at all." Your tongue might be bleeding, but you will be thankful later.

Marshall Goldsmith, recognized in 2011 as the most influential leadership thinker in the world by Harvard Business Review, is a firm believer that your words matter. He's a speaker, author, and an executive coach who coaches some of the world's top CEOs. Marshall fines his coaching clients $20 each time they use negative words such as "no," "but," and "however."

"Speak what you seek."

- Rick Holmberg

That money goes to their favorite nonprofit. At the time I heard him speak in 2013, he had raised over $900,000 for nonprofits on his clients' behalf. Marshall is also quick to point out that the $20 is not a financial hardship for his wealthy clients – it's more about the realization that they lost and couldn't adhere to seemingly simple standards.

What if you made slight changes to the words you speak?

Have to vs. Get to – Are you grateful for the places you get to go and the things you get to do every day or do you resent where you are spending your time? We can look at most things in life either as obligations (have to) or opportunities (get to). Maybe you have some opportunities that you have mislabeled as obligations. Very few things in life are truly obligations. Suppose your organization has a table at a fundraising event and you are asked to go to represent the organization. You might think of this as an obligation; what if you switched that perspective and viewed it as an opportunity? The words you speak will change your attitude and your expectations.

Next time you say, "I have to go to work." Think of someone who would be grateful to be in your situation – someone who is unemployed and would love to have a job.

Struggle vs. Challenge – Would you rather face a struggle or a challenge? A struggle implies an uphill battle against exhausting, defeating obstacles. A challenge, on the other hand, is something we can rise up to take.

Why is this happening to me vs. Why is this happening for me? – By changing one word in this question, we go from victim to overcomer.

Life is busy vs. Life is full – Busy often implies stress, and rushing for no reason, while having a full life, to me, is about getting intentional about what's in your life. **Is your but too big?** – You know it's coming. You can hear it in the tone of voice. Your friend says, "I've always wanted to do that, BUT ..."

Buts limit potential. What if you were able to look beyond the limitations and look toward creative solutions? What if you didn't have all the answers? What if you changed your habits and got rid of your excuses?

Buts validate inaction.

"I'd love to ... but now isn't the perfect time."

"I want to ... but I don't know how."

Buts negate praise.

"Great job today, BUT ..."

"You are a really nice person, BUT ..."

"You had some great plays today, BUT ..."

You can hear it in their tone. The affirming praise you are receiving is about to be negated by a big old but. Everything prior to the "but" is now erased. Why not use a period instead of the word but?

"Here's what I thought you did well."

"Here's how I think you could get even better."

It's a different conversation. Use a period. Or use the word "and." Have a better conversation.

Getting intentional about the words we use can help us appreciate our experiences and circumstances. The words we use impact our perspective on a situation.

What if you intentionally chose words that bring you hope, encouragement, peace, and joy? You know, words like ... hope, encouragement, peace and joy!

Before you speak, ask yourself if what you are about to say is going to add value to the conversation. You might just find yourself speaking less and listening more.

What You Read

Being on the radio in the morning has led me to pay attention to online news more often than I used to. If you have a pulse, you've probably noticed that most of the headlines are negative and many are actually disturbing. As we weed through the negative headlines to find the good news, I've found it very easy to get caught up in the "can you believe it" conversations. That's not very positive or uplifting, so I really have to work on staying focused on the good.

What we read shapes our view of the world. What we read can cause ideas to spark. What we read can change our life, if we let it. If you've made it this far in the book, you know this, and you know it's important to feed your mind good food. A friend who was mentored by Zig Ziglar told me that Zig's advice is to read a book 16 times before expecting it to sink in. 16 times. Keep on reading!

What You Listen To

You might be tempted to have the radio or TV on as background noise even though you aren't actively listening. You may not realize it, but the messages are sinking in. I've found myself absentmindedly singing along to many songs without having any idea what the song is all about. Once I stop and listen to the lyrics on some of the pop stations, I quickly realize I don't want THAT sinking into to my brain and I certainly don't want that for my kids either.

What You Watch

When I was a kid, my parents warned me not to watch scary movies before bed so I wouldn't have nightmares. Well, the same applies to the news! Overdose on any news outlet and guess what is infiltrating your brain? All the negativity, all the disturbing news. The U.S. Department of Veterans Affairs tells us that there is a link between watching news of traumatic events and elevated stress symptoms.*

If you're trying to lose weight yet you watch cooking shows with the latest and greatest desserts, it's not going to help your cause. However, if you're watching healthy cooking shows, now you're on to something. If you want more laughter in your life, watch a funny movie. If you want a good cry, snuggle up with a Hallmark movie and be prepared for the commercials to get you too.

Your Body Language

Your body language sends nonverbal messages to others about you. People make assumptions

*Source: National Center for PTSD www.ptsd.va.gov

about your mood, your confidence, your attentiveness, your frustration level and more based on your body language. Your body language can complement the words you speak or it can contradict the message you want to send. This piece of the communication puzzle is often overlooked. Start paying attention to your body language as you are in conversation with others.

Are your crossed arms conveying the fact that you are chilled or are others interpreting that pose as a sign that you are unreceptive or even argumentative?

Is your head nodding becoming a bobble-head syndrome? Men typically nod when they agree. They nod sparingly. Women often nod to indicate listening and encouragement, rather than agreement. In a business meeting, this can get comical; women doing the head-bobbing thing to show they are listening. Once you start looking for evidence of this – you will see it, and I hope you are able to stifle your giggles because it is pretty hilarious. Control the bobble-head!

Is your fidgeting sending a message of discomfort? Wringing your hands, repeatedly touching your neck or your jewelry, or fidgeting excessively will lead others to think you are uncomfortable with the role you are in or the topic being discussed.

The more you pay attention to your body

language and the body language of others, the more insight you will gain.

Your body language also impacts more than other people's impressions of you. It impacts your own level of confidence, as you'll see in the next section.

Your Confidence

It may seem like some people came out of the womb with confidence, but if that wasn't you, no worries. You can take steps to build your confidence. Maybe you felt confident at one time, but then life happened and you lost confidence, little by little, bit by bit. You can take steps to build your confidence.

Since we just talked about body language, let's go there again. Social psychologist Amy Cuddy researched body language and discovered this surprising truth: *our body language impacts our confidence.*

To increase our confidence, we should assume a "power pose." This is a pose where we take up a bit of space with our bodies instead of shrinking and minimizing ourselves. Imagine a runner crossing the finish line (arms up high and wide) or the confident stance of Wonder Woman - those are examples of a power pose. If you assume a power pose for at least two minutes, the physiology of your brain changes. Your cortisol (stress hormone) levels drop and your testosterone (a hormone often identified with leadership) levels rise. This physiological change brings about a state of increased confidence. Two minutes to increased confidence? Count me in!*

Other ways to increase your confidence:

Journal about positive experiences and milestones in your life

Keep a "feel-good" stash of notes received. Dig it out on those days when you need it.

Volunteer. When you serve others, you also help yourself.

Take baby steps toward something that is new and unfamiliar and a bit out of your comfort zone. Small victories can lead to big success.

Your Tone

If you're married or you're a parent, you get this.

Your tone of voice matters.

Their tone of voice matters.

Enough said.

Source: Your Body Language Shapes Who You Are, Amy Cuddy, www.ted.com

Your Emotions

Have you ever said, "He made me so mad, so I gave him a piece of my mind!"? Yeah? Me too. Let's talk about who is in control of our emotions and how we choose to respond based on our emotions. If you're a parent, you've probably coached your kids on this very topic. That's great! Now it's time to be real with yourself and hold the mirror up; are you in control of your emotions?

Replace judgment with curiosity

Controlling your emotions doesn't mean ignoring them or suppressing them. It's realizing that your emotions don't need to control you. Here are four steps to help you gain control:

1. The first step is always awareness. Start noticing those times your emotions get the best of you.

2. Change your perspective. Look at the situation from a variety of viewpoints, not just your own. What might have prompted the other person to say that, or behave in that way? Is there any chance you could be misinterpreting something?

3. Choose how you want to respond.

4. Find a healthy outlet to further process your emotions. Maybe it is sharing your situation with a friend (not ten friends, just one or two). Maybe it's journaling. Maybe it's releasing tension through exercise. Don't find just any outlet - find a healthy outlet.

STORY TIME

Joe was a manager at a sandwich deli, and he felt like his employees were out to get him. Not only did he take everything personally, but he was a perfectionist with very high expectations of others. When a situation didn't go his way, it was emotionally draining. After learning more about what he could control and shifting his perspective, Joe opened his mind to a new outlook for his work life and his home life. He learned that he didn't need to be conquered by fears, doubts, and personal demons. He became aware of what wasn't working, gained tools to make some changes and, most importantly, decided to change his perspective.

Who You Surround Yourself With

It's not too tough to figure out that if you are constantly surrounded by negative, bitter, or angry people, it will be more challenging for you to be positive. Choose to surround yourself with positive and uplifting people - virtually and in the real world.

A friend was dealing with some pretty major health issues, and she began seeing a naturopathic. One of the tasks he assigned her was to make a list of everyone she was in contact with during a two week period. Then, she was instructed to write a plus or minus sign by each person. If they added energy to her life, put a plus sign by their name. If they depleted energy from her, put a minus by their name. Then, she was to spend as much time as possible with the "positive" people and minimize or eliminate time with the "negative" people.

People are like elevators; they either lift you up or bring you down.

Maybe some of the people in your life are negative and draining, yet due to circumstances outside of your control, you must spend time with them. Make an intentional effort to stay focused on what you can control; there's no need to be receptive to their negativity.

Viktor Frankl, a concentration camp survivor and author of Man's Search for Meaning stated: "When we are no longer able to change a situation, we are challenged to change ourselves."

Your Busy-ness

If you are busy, what are you busy doing? Is it a good busy or a stressed busy? Listening to water cooler conversations would almost have me believe that busy has become a badge of honor. Is busy the goal?

> The illusion of busy can keep us from pursuing our dreams and making an impact in the world.

One of the saddest conversations I've had was in passing with a business colleague in a hallway at a sporting event. Hindsight is 20/20, so I didn't know how disheartening this exchange was at the time. The quick hallway conversation went like this:

Me: "Hi Sharon, good to see you, how are you?"

Sharon: "Busy."

Me: "Busy good? Busy stressful?"

Sharon: "So busy I feel like my life is passing me by."

Me: "I'm sorry to hear that ..."

And that was the end of the interaction as we were both going to watch the next game. I didn't reach out to Sharon with a phone call or an email, yet the interaction stuck with me. I regret

White space on the calendar is a blessing. Cherish the white space.

that decision immensely. About two months after this hallway interaction, I heard the tragic news that Sharon's life had been taken from her. A busy life was passing her by, and now that life had ended. Tears still come to my eyes as I think of her and wonder who else is feeling like life is passing them by?

None of us know where we are on the timeline of life. It's easy to think we've got years and years to live life fully, but what if that's not the case for you or for me?

Age/Life Expectancy = x/12 a.m. - 11:59 p.m.

Here's an eye-opening formula, and this one actually involves math. Last week I had a conversation with a friend about evaluating our age compared to our life expectancy, so we can see what percent of our journey we might (statistically speaking) have left. Then, if we take that further and equate our life span to a 24 hour day, it gets the heart pumping! Check it out ...

The latest life expectancy figure for a female in the U.S. is 81 years. Right now, I'm 46, so I've already lived 56.7% of my life, according to the stats. Equating that percentage to a 24 hour day, if my math is right (and, don't worry, I had someone else double-check it), I'm already at 1:30 p.m. on my journey to midnight.

For me, that creates a sense of urgency!

Faith Over Fear

Are you coming from a place of faith or a place of fear?

Several years ago, we went to the Rainforest Cafe in the Mall of America. Our daughters were about five and two at the time. We were seated in a prime location with the gorillas right above our table. Soon the animation started; the gorillas started moving and the booms of "thunder" along with a variety of animal noises filled the restaurant. I turned to our two-year-old to see her reaction, only to realize she was no longer in her chair! Excitement gave way to panic until we looked under the table and, thank God, there she was, hiding from the storm and the crazy gorillas.

For God gave us a spirit not of fear but of power and love and self-control.

2 Timothy 1:7 (ESV)

When the inevitable storms of life come, what do you do? Do you hide under the table in fear? Don't let fear cause you to miss out or retreat. Choose faith over fear.

We fear so much in this world: losing a loved one, the safety of our children, losing our job, failure, losing our health, gaining weight, the sales quota, dwindling retirement funds, health care, the economy, and the list goes on.

A fear of tomorrow does not allow us to be present to enjoy today. When we are in fear mode, we can become paralyzed with insecurity. Think of how we respond to situations when we are in fear mode - anger, anxiety, withdrawal, worry, dread. These are some pretty unhealthy emotions! Just as you cannot think a positive thought and a negative thought simultaneously, neither can you be living in faith while fearing tomorrow.

"Feed your fears and your faith will starve. Feed your faith and your fears will."

- Max Lucado

I have been blessed with the opportunity to meet many amazing people along my journey. No one has ever told me that a best practice is to live in fear and allow it to prevent action. There will be peaks and valleys. Know that, expect it, but don't let fear overtake you and prevent you from moving forward.

What if you lived by faith not fear? It doesn't mean you won't have any more challenges - the challenges will still be there – but you will be far better equipped to handle those challenges when you operate from a faith-based mindset.

Do you have the courage to proceed with the mindset of faith, believing your best days are not behind you but ahead of you? Knowing and believing this, and taking purposeful action, you will make the right choices today that will create your positive future tomorrow. You will focus on solutions rather than problems. You will continue to invest in your organization, your people and yourself. You will stay calm, focused and committed to your vision and purpose. You look for ways to save money and reduce expenses without making irrational fear-based decisions that sacrifices your future success. You find the opportunities in the challenges. Your faith can then become contagious and you impact others through your belief. Think of the impact this can have on your family, your organization, your team, and your clients.

Fear will always be around the corner. Don't go there. Living with purpose and passion means living with faith. Go there.

Your Priorities

Our family loves to pull out our cowboy boots and hats and go horseback riding. Since we don't own horses, we occasionally go to riding stables to get our horse fix. When the girls were seven and ten, we decided to go for a morning ride at a stable near our lake cabin. The girls were super excited, but their excitement gave way to frustration as their focus turned to who was wearing which cowboy hat. The prior year, they had each gotten a new cowboy hat - one was pink and one was orange. Yes, pink and orange cowboy hats. I certainly didn't recall whose was whose, and apparently there was a trade that occurred at some point over the winter. Well, there we were, trying to get on the road on time and the girls were arguing about who gets the pink cowboy hat.

When you focus on what's really important, everything else falls into place.

Seriously! I recall trying to interject with the voice of reason about how insignificant the argument was, but it fell on deaf ears. In fact, the arguing escalated and my husband issued an ultimatum: quit arguing and get in the car or we wouldn't be going horseback riding! (Ouch, that would have been punishment for me, too.)

Thankfully, the girls understood how serious we were, so the arguing stopped and we were on our way. When we got to the stables, we were welcomed by the owner of the stable. What she said as she greeted the girls was priceless: "Girls, you look adorable in your cowboy hats, but you won't be able to wear them - we require riding helmets."

Has that ever happened to you? Have you ever lost sight of the main thing? Have you ever lost sight of what's truly important? Think of the workaholic who claims his family is the most important thing, yet he's at the office 15 hours a day. Actions speak louder than words.

Your Engagement in Work, in Life

Do you remember those employee engagement stats at the beginning of the book? If you are employed and you're surprised at these numbers, you are probably among the few, the proud, the engaged 30%. Congratulations! Engaged employees are having more fun at work! They are contributing to the mission of the organization; they are inspired, passionate, productive, and intentional.

The sad reality is that the majority of the workforce is either disengaged or *actively* disengaged. Given the amount of hours we spend at work, wouldn't we rather be engaged? And, it is way more fun when your co-workers are engaged and, by default, not slacking off. If your co-workers aren't engaged, you are probably carrying some of their workload.

If you're a leader in your organization, wouldn't you rather have a team who is engaged? Of course. You'll have better synergy, better client service and all-around better results.

The big blaring news here is that employee engagement is not the leader's responsibility. It's not the human resource department's responsibility. It is your responsibility. Maybe you don't envision yourself at your current job for much longer – that's fine, but why not make the most of the time you are there and don't be "that guy" who quits working before he resigns.

If you are not feeling engaged, start re-engaging:

Connect your role to the bigger picture. What value do you provide? Who are you impacting?

Learn something new.

Look for ways to create efficiencies or solve problems in your department.

Set a stretch goal.

Quit complaining. Quit worrying. Focus on the positive.

Talk to your supervisor about how you can grow in your role or assist in other areas.

What about your engagement in your life and the lives of your family members and friends? Are you living life or are you retreating in front of a screen or other distraction? Life can be challenging, especially during certain stages of life, and it can be easy to retreat and disengage. That disengagement, though, could lead to more challenges.

Do Your Part

"Why am I here?" That was the subject line of an email from my new client, Joe. He was 58 years old and in a job he didn't enjoy. He wasn't excited to get up every day. Retirement was several years into the future, as the past recession had taken a toll on his financial situation. Knowing he had several years left to work, he knew he needed a change, and he really wanted to find something he enjoyed. In his view, though, he couldn't imagine anyone hiring him because he of his age.

During a coaching session, I encouraged Joe to reach out to some of his connections and let them know confidentially that he was looking for a new opportunity. In my experience, every step creates momentum, and steps like this are critical to create momentum.

Sure enough, one of the business owners he met with told Joe his company was looking for an international sales manager and encouraged Joe to apply. Joe told me about their conversation and then proceeded to tell me that he didn't think he was qualified for the position, so he likely wouldn't apply.

You do your part. Let God do His.

Obviously, that didn't sit well with me! I told Joe we all have to do our part. It was up to him to apply for the position. It was up to the HR department and God to determine if he got the job.

So, he did. He applied for the job and prayed. In fact, his prayer contained a bit of a timeline. *And, God, if you could let me know by noon on Friday what my future is, that would be great.*

Guess what? He got the call for an interview that Friday morning and he subsequently got the job! And, of course the company provided him with connections and resources to equip him to do the job. Now he is starting out each day with more energy and purpose than he had experienced for years.

You have to do your part!

Otherwise life will pass you by.

Create Your Own Definitions

Picture yourself at the end of your long and wonderful life. What would a life by design look like for you? You get to create what that looks like. Success is whatever you define it to be. This might require a bit of thought. Some measure success as raising kids to be productive adults, others quantify success related to the impact they are making on the community or the world, or a job title, job longevity, financial status, etc. You may have multiple measurements of success in your life. Your definition of success doesn't have to equal anyone else's definition of success.

Many say happiness is fleeting. Yet when we ask those same people what they want for their kids, they say happiness. Call it happiness, joy, satisfaction, meaning, fulfillment, peace, or whatever you prefer. It's a feeling – a state of being – that you strive for. You get to decide what that looks like for you.

LET GO OF THE REST

Now that we've figured out what we can control and have some insight on how to take control, let's switch gears.

Obviously, there's a lot we can't control and never will be able to control. For years, I believed

I was good at this "letting go" dimension but once I really evaluated it, I realized I still had work to do.

What causes us to hold on tighter and want to control the uncontrollable? We are faced with constant change, economic uncertainty, rapidly changing technology, physical clutter, mental clutter, complex processes, commitments, and on and on. The more out of control we feel, the more we want to control something ... anything! Have you ever gone through a challenging time with lots of changes in your environment, and you were actually excited to go home and clean the house or the garage? For most of us, cleaning isn't fun, but it is controllable, predictable, and you can see the results.

Q: What is the risk of holding on too tightly?

A: Stress

A cover story in Time magazine in 1983 called stress "The Epidemic of the Eighties" and referred to it as the leading health problem of the decade; I have a sneaking suspicion that our stress levels have increased since 1983.

A bit of stress can be good; it can provide a sense of urgency and stimulate us to take action. It's the ongoing, unrelenting stress that we don't know how to deal with that can cause problems. The American Institute of Stress estimates that

75% to 90% of all visits to primary care physicians are for stress-related problems. There is a direct correlation between your mind and your body. Mental and emotional stress will eventually show up in your body. The good news in this is that we can take steps to reduce our stress.

It isn't about what happens to you, it is about how you respond to what happens to you.

Think about all the things you worry about that you are unable to control. Perhaps you worry about the economy, the future of our nation, the weather (especially in the upper Midwest), the price of gas, and what THEY will think. *Quick question: who are THEY and why do you care?*

Let me ask you something: Do you have time and energy to spare? I didn't think so. Then why waste your precious energy on situations and people you cannot control?

It's none of your business what other people think of you.

What We Gain by Letting Go

When we let go, we gain peace of mind, improved health, and better relationships! No more giving your family the leftovers. I'm a big fan of leftovers in the fridge, but too often we give our family the leftovers of us. We've dished out everything we can during the day, and there is nothing left for those who we say are the most important people in our lives. We've all heard that we should give 110% on the job and "leave it all on the field." I was delighted to hear Albert Tate share his view at the 2015 Global Leadership Summit that if we give too much at work, we will be depleted for our families. Doing your best is absolutely critical, but leaving it all on the field with nothing left for your family is likely to cause problems on the homefront.

Once we start getting intentional with our lives, we spend energy on what matters so we can accomplish the great things we were put on earth to do.

Worrying about what you can't control wastes energy; focus on what you can control.

That's all great, but how do we let go? First, become aware of what you are doing and then make an intentional effort to change. It sounds simple, but it isn't always easy. Take baby steps: delegate, say no, ask for help, and work to eliminate your desire for perfection.

Other People and Their Choices

We spend a lot of time and energy trying to control other people. You can influence others, absolutely, but control them? Just let it go. You'll be happier, and they will, too.

What would happen if I let my co-worker run the meeting? What if I'm more focused on the end result and less focused on the exact approach he uses? What if I let the kids do their own laundry? What if I didn't have to have my closet perfect and color coded? (A meaningful life is still do-able with a messy closet – been there, done that, still doing that.)

When Alyssa was in third grade, her teacher told us it was a great age to let her take responsibility for her homework and her schedule. We took that advice to heart, and our girls have become responsible and independent. That can be tough love sometimes; if they forgot their homework at home, it didn't necessarily mean we brought it to them. As kids grow up, it's okay to let them experience the consequences of their actions.

If we let go, our employees, our co-workers, and our kids will be more accountable, more empowered and less micromanaged.

Weapons of Mass Destruction

Our minds are often storage facilities for Weapons of Mass Destruction (WMD):

W = Worry
M = Misery
D = Despair

We must be ready with offensive and defensive maneuvers to avoid attacks from these types of weapons. The WMD we're talking about are those which we can control. If we don't take control of them, they can be detrimental with long-term negative consequences.

The fact is, we live in a world with actual weapons, real threats, pain, and suffering. We don't need to magnify those realities by giving in to worry, misery, or despair. You may think you are the only one ...

- who is uncertain of what tomorrow will bring.

- who doesn't feel qualified to tackle that project.

- who doesn't feel equipped to take on that role.

- who is going through what you are going through.

You are not the only one! We've all, at one point or another, faced similar fears, doubts, and challenges. You may be tempted to succumb to a life of teary movies and tissues, or hiding out in the mancave. Some people allow themselves to be crippled by worry, misery, and despair; others choose to overcome and persevere in spite of the temptation to give in and give up.

Be the one who chooses to overcome and persevere!

A friend, who is also self-employed, once said, "I just want to get to the point in my business where I don't have to worry about my income in the next several months." I can relate to that. If you've ever been self-employed, you can probably relate to that, too. That feeling that she is referring to is a state of mind. Whether or not she worries about the future won't change the future. Let's take worry out of the equation and just focus on the choices we can control.

Blame/Victim Mentality

Not only do we worry about things we can't control, but we like to blame the world, our family, the boss, for holding us back or for things not turning out the way we wanted. It's easy to be a victim and blame other people for our circumstances. It's a greater challenge to overcome blame and become accountable.

How about you? Do you view your past experiences as a school that prepares you for the future or are you bound by those experiences like a prison? If you are full of excuses for why you can't do this, or why that never works for you, you might be a victim. You might be bound by the past.

Let your past be a school not a prison.

All the Rest That Doesn't Serve You

Judgment

Being right

Excuses

Anger

Bitterness

Resentment

Envy

Fear

Bad habits

Comparisons

Unrealistic expectations of others

Unrealistic expectations of yourself

Excuses

Guilt

Too much concern about what other people think

Can we agree that worrying about things we can't control consumes our energy, increases our stress, impairs our health, and damages relationships? Let it go!

Letting it Go

That's all fine and dandy, but how do you let it go? There are five critical words that can help you let go:

It is what it is."

While participating in a mastermind group, this was a phrase often repeated by a few people in the room. In fact, one woman even had a t-shirt that said, "It is what it is." I really thought the phrase was over-used and a bit dismissive. Then one day I finally realized ... it is what it is! If you can't change a situation, don't waste time and effort trying to change it. Accept it and move on. This is not a pass

"It is what it is. And, it becomes what you make it."

- Scott Shickler

for people to be jerks and treat others miserably, and it's not an easy out for you to avoid dealing with a situation you can and should deal with. This phrase is for those times when you know you need to let something go because you can't change it.

Continually focus on what's within your control. If you can control it, take control of it! If you cannot control it/them, pray about it/them, wish them well, and move on.

PARTING
THOUGHTS

DON'T "SHOULD" ON YOURSELF OR ANYONE ELSE

How many times have you been told "You should..." or "You shouldn't ..."? As a parent, I know that phrase is sometimes warranted. You shouldn't touch a hot stove - true! When we are "shoulding" on ourselves (or someone else is "shoulding" on us), we must test it to make sure it is something that we really want to do. If someone tells you "you should get that college degree" ... should you? You have to test it to make sure it fits for you. Make sure it's your decision, not a fulfillment of someone else's expectations of you.

A LIFE OF NO REGRETS?

A life of no regrets sounds like a worthy ideal. However, we are human, and we make mistakes.

I don't know about you, but ...

I've done things I wish I hadn't.

I haven't done things I wish I had.

I've said things I shouldn't say.

I haven't said the things I should say.

With age, wisdom, and intentionality, I believe we can have less regrets, but I think it's an unrealistic goal to strive for a life of no regrets. Forgive yourself and others for things done and left undone, and move forward knowing tomorrow is a new day.

JUST FOR TODAY (AND TOMORROW, TOO)

Zig Ziglar said, "People say motivation doesn't last. Neither does bathing; that's why we recommend it daily." It is a daily choice to determine your attitude, and how you are going to respond to whatever comes your way during the day.

WHAT IF YOU WANT TO GIVE UP?

You may have moments, days or even weeks when you feel like giving up. You might think it would be easier to just stay where you are; after all, our comfort zones can be really comfortable. When I feel like giving up, I ask myself, "Will I regret not giving it one more shot?" If I know I'll have regrets, then it makes it easier to keep going. Conversations with friends on similar journeys are critical when you want to give up. They all make it look so easy, yet when we have a heart-to-heart, we both discover how similar our challenges are.

How can you keep going when things get tough?

Connect with a friend. That can give you the encouragement to keep on going.

Take a "fun" break; do something you love that energizes you.

Take time to relax and recharge.

Connect with others who are on a similar path, and you'll be reminded that you're not alone.

EVERY STEP CREATES MOMENTUM

You know that momentum helps achieve results. When you lose momentum, projects stall, creativity is stifled, and future results are jeopardized. The "48 hour rule" is one way for you to keep momentum going.

If you operate with the 48 hour rule in mind, it means you follow-up or take action within 48 hours of the opportunity, idea, or instinct to act. You make a plan to act within 48 hours after interest has been established. After 48 hours momentum is lost. Distractions abound. New problems are vying for your attention.

Have you ever left a conference or a meeting with great action ideas but on the way to your office, you got side-tracked? Then a customer called, then it was time for lunch, then ... time slips away and the excitement is gone and momentum is lost.

Have you ever had a random thought to call someone that you hadn't seen for months? Take action and make the call! You might be just the person they need to hear from.

Be careful not to get too hung up on your plans and your timetables. Let your *WHY* drive you not the *HOW*. *WHY* you do what you do matters. *HOW* you get there will likely be a different path than you envisioned.

When we get too attached to the outcome/the result/the how, then we are holding on too tightly.

Your job is to take the next step.

And, after that, look for the next step and take it. See how that works?

Commit now to taking a step forward within 48 hours. It can be one step in the right direction; it doesn't have to involve a huge undertaking. Every step creates momentum. Momentum toward your best life; a life by design.

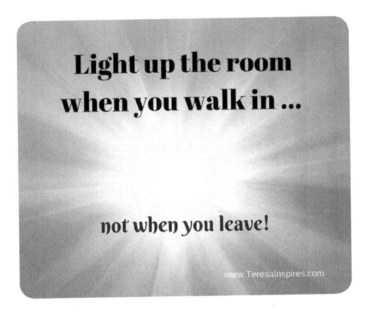

Light up the room
when you walk in ...

not when you leave!

www.TeresaInspires.com

WHAT'S NEXT?

GET CONNECTED AND GET INSPIRED!

Get connected and get inspired on social media @TeresaInspires

Elevate your results by working with me 1:1, or bring me to your organization or conference for a big dose of inspiration!

Learn more: www.TeresaInspires.com

THE LIFE BY DESIGN THINKBOOK

If you've ever attended a group exercise class, you know that the instructor gives guidance for the basic exercise, and then she follows it up with, "If you want more…" That is where the next level comes in. I get pretty excited when I can do the next step without injury or catastrophe! Thankfully, the next step I'm talking about here is definitely catastrophe-free and can accelerate your journey to your best life.

In my experience, much can be gained by taking time to evaluate and reflect, and that's exactly what the Life by Design ThinkBook does. It's a series of activities and questions designed to help you gain clarity and move forward.

Do you want to take yourself to the next level? Are you ready to be all in? Go online and purchase the Life by Design Thinkbook, available at www.TeresaInspires.com. The ThinkBook contains questions to help you reflect on where you are, where you want to go and why. This is a great resource for a personal journey into a life by design or it could set the stage for some meaningful discussions in your book club.

APPENDIX

APPENDIX A: THE FINE PRINT

Failure to be intentional about your life could result in dissatisfaction, disillusion, grouchiness, loss of friends, and general isolation, and is not recommended for normal human beings.

You should not embrace an intentional lifestyle if you enjoy being crabby now, have always been crabby, have no intent not to be crabby, and are just crabby, crabby period.

There are possible side effects from choosing to live this way and they include:

Strange glances from friends and family as they notice the changes in you.

Some people report more energy.

In most people, there is a definite increase in peace and contentment.

There may be occasional outbursts of joy.

This lifestyle may increase your risk of more smile wrinkles (and, of course, there is a drug for that).

APPENDIX B: LIFE IS TOO SHORT TO...

Life is too short to focus on being right rather than being happy.

Human beings have this urge to be right and let our ego dance in victory! But, what is "right"? "Right" is what we make of it in our own mind. It is only a matter of perspective, and there are just as many perspectives as there are people in this world. That bears repeating: There are just as many perspectives as there are people in this world. You can easily change your perspective by getting out of your box – helping someone, volunteering, doing something you've never done, going someplace you've never been. Then pay attention to the conversations around you. Odds are, you might be enlightened, and you may gain a different perspective and new appreciation for the unfamiliar.

Life is too short to say yes to everything.

We have limited time on this earth, and we are reminded of that every day. We've got 168 hours in a week, and we really could benefit by thinking about what we allow to occupy those hours. The word "no" is in the dictionary and people actually use it. Sometimes you have to say "no" to others in order to say "yes" to yourself.

I've continually had several opportunities to say "no" to wonderful causes. I would love to help out in every way and every situation, yet my life is quite full. I've realized that at this stage of life, when I say "yes" to someone else, I'm actually saying "no" to my family.

Life is too short to believe everything you think.

For years, you've been filling your mind with all sorts of thoughts that may or may not be true. Test everything you think. Challenge everything you think. If you aren't 100% certain it is absolute truth, change that thought.

Life is too short to sweat the small stuff.

We've all heard it before, but do we live it? Suzy Welch, wife of former GE CEO Jack Welch, recommends using the 10/10/10 rule. Will it matter in ten minutes, ten months or ten years? Act accordingly.

Life is too short to iron (at least for me)!

This is especially endearing when pronounced in the five-year-old "I-run" version. When Alyssa was five, she saw an ironing board at grandma's house and asked what it was. Grandma, appalled, said, "You must be joking!" No, grandma, no joke, Alyssa had never seen an ironing board! Why? Because I've discovered that it is way easier to iron wrinkles *in* than iron wrinkles *out,* and, frankly, a few minutes after you wear it, you can't tell it's been ironed anyway! If it were at all therapeutic, I would consider it, but for me, it is more likely to push me into therapy. No judgment – if you enjoy ironing, then iron away!

Life is too short to wear matched socks!

Okay, this isn't my "thing," but I have heard this story about a local business man. My friend saw him on a few occasions well-dressed in a suit and tie and ... mismatched socks! When questioned, he indicated that life is really too short to spend time rummaging around the sock drawer to find a pair, so now he just buys similar socks and mixes them. Obviously a conversation-starter. Obviously a time-saver. Yes, I know a few of you are appalled and could never leave the bedroom, let alone the house, with mismatched socks. My challenge: I dare you. See what conversations spark and let me know.

APPENDIX C: THE FLIGHT ATTENDANTS HAVE IT RIGHT

If you've flown, you've heard the flight attendants say, "Put on your own oxygen mask first." Boy, do they have it right. We have to take care of ourselves in order to be a blessing to others.

We must take care of our bodies to be able to function at our best, and to give the world the best of us. When it comes to our health, we have to realize that everything is a choice and we need to start owning our choices.

What price are you willing to pay to maintain your health now? If you don't pay the price now, you can bet you will pay it later - at a much higher price.

What do you eat? Are you fueling your body with the nutrition it needs? Are you getting through the day thanks to sugar and caffeine? If you say you want to shed pounds, yet you order a combination meal, plus pop, plus dessert, do you really want to shed those pounds?

Take time to take care of yourself. It's not selfish, it's self-care.

What do you drink? Is what you drink fueling your body or contaminating your body?

How much physical activity do you get every day? The demands of work and full schedules often lead us to believe we don't have time to take care of ourselves. Furthermore, many of us are at our computers every day for hours at a time. This sedentary lifestyle is not good for our health.

Do you want to get healthier? Start hanging out with people who have healthy lifestyles. Read articles about healthy living. Listen to podcasts focused on health. And, make choices that reflect your intent.